Fir

Introduction

It's now over 14 years since Peter Ha … le' to Goa and much has changed since then. The hip … thousands of package holidaymakers, not just fr … arts of India. Consequently the coastal strip, in particular has seen considerable development yet, despite this, many of the best sites have continued to be productive for birders. It's true that some, such as 'Ciba-Geigy' and the Merck dump are now almost useless but in other ways Goa has become an even better place for birders to visit.

This is largely due to the rise of local enterprises that make it much easier to connect with the birds you might want to see. Firstly there are now 'taxi-drivers-cum-bird-guides' who will pick you up from your hotel, take you to the bird sites and even find and identify the birds for you; secondly there is an excellent boat-trip up the river Zuari with a boatman who knows just where to find many otherwise difficult species and, lastly, you shouldn't miss the fantastic 'Backwoods' camp where you can spend two or three nights in the forests of the Western Ghats in the company of knowledgeable, enthusiastic local guides who ensure that you'll see most of the specialities, including many endemics.

Hence, instead of wandering around on your own, struggling to see even half of the available species, all you need to do is take advantage of this local expertise. It might be said that with their help, you don't need a site guide such as this but here, in one place, with clear, detailed maps, is all the information you need to help you plan your trip, make the most of the areas you can walk to, decide which sites to ask to be taken to, and have a better idea of what to look for at each site. If you are unable to get one of the best taxi-drivers, or if you want to explore the area on your own, I hope you'll find this book especially useful. You could prepare for your trip by hunting through lots of trip reports on the internet and maybe printing off lots of descriptions of the same places but I hope you find this book to be a much more convenient 'one-stop shop' that you can easily take with you when you go.

You're bound to have a great time.

Dave Gosney,
April 2010

Acknowledgements

The information in this book is based on my own experiences in Goa, greatly assisted by expert guides such as Santosh Redkar and the Backwoods team (Leio, Loven and Pramod) as well as much information gleaned from trip reports by Mark and Sandra Dennis, Rhion Pritchard, Ray Thorneycroft, Paul Wetton, Mark Easterbrook, Brian Eady, Roy Ticehurst, Steve Baines, Chris Johnson and Phil Ramsgate, all accessed via the internet. Thanks too to Terry and Carole Spooner, Dave Sanderson, Paul and Em Pearson and Alistair and Jilda Miller for their company on some of my days in Goa. Lastly most thanks must go to my partner Liz whose camerawork, editing and designing are essential to this project and who also provides the most wonderful company on all these trips.

North Goa

This book only covers the birding sites in North Goa (north of the Zuari river which splits the state in two). This is because most birders stay in the Baga area and very few visit the south; it's possible to see just about all the best birds of Goa without including sites in the south such as the Cotigao National Park and Velim Lake.

The common birds of Goa

Wherever you stay in Goa, you should be able to find some 'back lanes' in which to wander in search of birds. In leafy, wooded areas, including gardens and hotel grounds, you should find birds such as Green(ish) Warbler (call: 'chewysup' like Pied Wagtail), Indian Golden Oriole, Asian Koel, Tailorbird, Coppersmith Barbet (call: a far-carrying, hollow 'whup, whup'), White-cheeked Barbet (call: a loud 'ka-tok, ka-tok'), Ring-necked Parakeet, Plum-headed Parakeet, Purple-rumped Sunbird and the ubiquitous House Crows. In more open areas you'll find Indian Magpie Robin, Pied Chat, Spotted Dove, White-browed Wagtail, Jungle Myna, Indian Roller, Little Green Bee-eater, Wire-tailed Swallow, Black Drongo, Long-tailed Shrike, Cattle Egret and White-breasted Kingfisher. There will always be kites in the air, both Black and Brahminy but keep checking them and you should also get both Oriental (Crested) Honey-buzzard and White-bellied Sea Eagle. Wherever there's water, you can also expect Little and Intermediate Egrets, Indian Pond Heron, Red-wattled Lapwing and Common Kingfisher and a walk through any grassy fields should produce pipits, usually Paddyfield Pipits. After that, you'll need to work a bit harder, travel around to the sites in this book and/or get the help of a local guide.

Hiring a guide

Lots of taxi-drivers will offer to show you birds. Most of them know at least some of the best sites and may even offer to show you roosting owls and nightjars at well-known stake-outs. But you will get a far more rewarding experience if you find a guide who is able to identify every bird you see or hear. In many cases, the best guides charge pretty much the same as other taxi-drivers so it would be crazy not to use them. On my last two visits I spent several days with Santosh Redkar who has a well-deserved reputation as possibly the best of the local guides. Apart from being pleasant company and reassuringly reliable he also knows the birds well, has a phenomenal ability to find stuff and has a few of his own 'special sites' (eg for Indian Pitta) that most other drivers don't know. Other taxi drivers with good reputations include 'Raymond' and Mahesh. Another, Lloyd Fernandes, now runs a more up-market, but more expensive, operation called 'birds and breakfast' which includes travel in his minibus. To find Santosh you could ask for him outside the Beira Mar hotel in Baga or you can phone him on 9881180424 or email him in advance at goabirdingsantosh@hotmail.com.

When to go

The consensus view is that the months of November to February are best for birding. From March onwards the weather gets increasingly hot until the monsoon season of August to October when sapping humidity makes for uncomfortable birding. The post-monsoon season from November onwards should be the best time as birds are at their most active but I'll just add a warning that, in 2009, the monsoon season was exceptionally late, continuing well into November; the high humidity continued at Backwoods until about the 23rd of the month. Hence November should be the perfect time, but there is an element of risk that it may not be.

Baga/Arpora area

Attraction

This is where most birdwatchers stay, principally because of the variety of productive habitats (marshes, saltpans, fields and woods) all within walking distance of a number of hotels. The most favoured hotels for birders are the Beira Mar, next to a freshwater marsh and the Marinha Dourada, next to some great saltpans. The Marinha Dourada is further from the coast but is blissfully separated from the heaving mass of tourists and traffic that has turned Baga/Calangute/Candolim into a place to be avoided. It is also much better located for walking to Baga Hill or Arpora Woods. The Riverside Regency is a cheaper alternative – it has a pleasant location at the foot of Baga Hill, is just a 20-minute walk from both of the key wetlands and perfect for Baga fields.

Getting there

The transfer from the airport can take 1-3 hours depending on the number of 'drop-offs' to be made.

Access

Feel free to wander freely throughout this area, but show the usual respect for privacy and fenced off sites. In 2007-08, the tracks to Baga Hill east and Arpora Woods had signs saying 'Trespassers will be prosecuted' but the word was that they had no legitimacy so they were ignored by birders. By 2009 the signs had gone.

Notes

1. Many rooms at the Marinha Dourada hotel (15.5681N, 73.7608E) overlook a saline lake but this is typically birdless, apart from a Striated Heron which feeds there, especially around the waterfall feature next to the sunbeds. The open sky above the lake is well-worth scanning for birds such as Little Swift, Oriental Honey-buzzard, White-bellied Sea Eagle and three species of parakeet including Alexandrine.

2. The saltpans immediately across the road from the Marinha Dourada hotel offer a bonanza of birds, unless the water levels are unusually high or low. Amongst many herons you should get a chance to compare Great White and Intermediate Egrets and you should see 4 species of kingfisher including Pied and Stork-billed. A wide range of waders is likely to include many familiar species plus Marsh Sandpiper and Temminck's Stint. Small Pratincole and Broad-billed Sandpiper are also seen regularly (up to 200 of the former). Around the pools, look for Spotted Dove, Pied Chat, Paddyfield Pipit, Blue-tailed Bee-eater, Ashy Wood-swallow, Rose-coloured and Chestnut-tailed Starlings and the uncommon Common Myna.

3. Baga Hill is an easy walk from either the Marinha Dourada or the Riverside Regency and offers some 'real' Indian birds such as Puff-throated Babbler, Small Minivet, Indian Bush Chat, Common Peafowl, Red Spurfowl, prinias, leafbirds etc. (see page 7 for more details)

4. There's a site for nesting and roosting Alexandrine Parakeets near the Marinha Dourada. Take the road north from the Mojo's bar and keep going, past the Sun Village hotel, through the next village until you see an obvious bridge over the river on your right. The parakeets roost and nest in the walled palm plantation on the far side of the river (15.5765N, 73.7593E) and can also be seen by the roadside a little

further on. En route to the plantation you'll pass a pool which in 2009 had a few waders including Pacific Golden Plover. The commoner Rose-ringed (=Ring-necked) Parakeets occur here too.

5. Arpora Woods can be even better for birds than Baga Hill but is still within easy walking distance of the Marinha Dourada. You'll get lots of 'extra' species here but the most sought after birds include Indian Pitta, Rufous Woodpecker and Blue-faced Malkoha (see page 8 for more details).

6. Baga fields are good for birds of open country such as as pipits, munias, starlings, rollers and drongos. There are two main points of access: the most popular one is 250 metres south of Baga bridge where a path leads north-east (15.5634N, 73.7518E) past a small pool. It is also possible to access the fields by walking outside the northern perimeter of the Beira Mar hotel as far as the 'Bittern Pool' (15.5578N, 73.7571E) and finding a route out from there. By walking around the grassy areas you are likely to flush a few pipits, snipe and possibly Quail. Paddyfield is the most widespread pipit but you should also find Richard's and Blyth's Pipits. Both Pintail and Eurasian Snipe occur but Pintail is perhaps the more common. I haven't identified the quail I've seen here but Rock Bush Quail was reported in 2002. Other species to look for include (un)Common Myna, Malabar Lark, Hoopoe and Chestnut-tailed Starling and it's a great spot for photographing common birds such as Indian Roller, Long-tailed Shrike and Black Drongo. Other birds reported here in recent years have included Bay-backed Shrike, Brahminy Starling, Eurasian (not Indian) Roller, Watercock, Indian Silverbill and Yellow-wattled Lapwing.

7. These raised mounds (15.5651N, 73.7534E) have lines of bushes which attract species such as Scaly-breasted Munia and, at least at passage times, Yellow-breasted Buntings.

8. The Beira Mar hotel offers birders unique opportunities to get close views of marsh birds. The key birds to look for, much easier here than anywhere else, are Greater Painted-snipe, Cinnamon Bittern and Ruddy-breasted Crake. The crake and the Painted-snipe are best looked for in the evening around the open channel by the bushes to the right as you look out from the swimming pool verandah but they may not appear until it is practically dark. The Cinnamon Bittern also waits until nightfall before it begins to stalk the 'Bittern Pool' below the next verandah (to the left, on the other side of the toilet block). Other birds likely to be seen well include Clamorous Reed Warbler (immediately over the fence) and Pintail Snipe (with a chance of comparing them side-by-side with Common Snipe). Further out on the marsh, look out for Purple Heron, Rosy and Chestnut-tailed Starlings, White-rumped and Black-headed Munias, Baya Weavers and various raptors including Marsh and, sometimes, Pallid Harriers. Other birds seen here in the past have included Paddyfield Warbler, Bluethroat, Streaked Weaver, Ashy Wood Swallow, Baillon's Crake, Spotted Crake, Slaty-breasted Rail, Purple Swamphen, Watercock, Black-capped Kingfisher and Yellow Bittern. You don't have to stay at the hotel to enjoy these birds; non-residents are welcome to visit as long as they spend some money while they're there. To find the pool, walk down the lane to the Beira Mar (from 15.5574N, 73.7556E) and look for a track to the left of reception, signposted to the Paradise Restaurant. In November 2009 I was unable to see most of the waterbirds; this may reflect a deterioration of the marsh or may have been due to the exceptionally high water levels of that time.

9. Many of the raptors that soar over Baga Hill can be viewed from the Riverside Regency hotel. It is also possible to look out into trees from the balconies of the rooms and see species such as Indian Golden Oriole, Green Warbler, Blue-winged Leafbird, Asian Brown Flycatcher, Ashy Drongo, Plain Flowerpecker and Coppersmith Barbet.

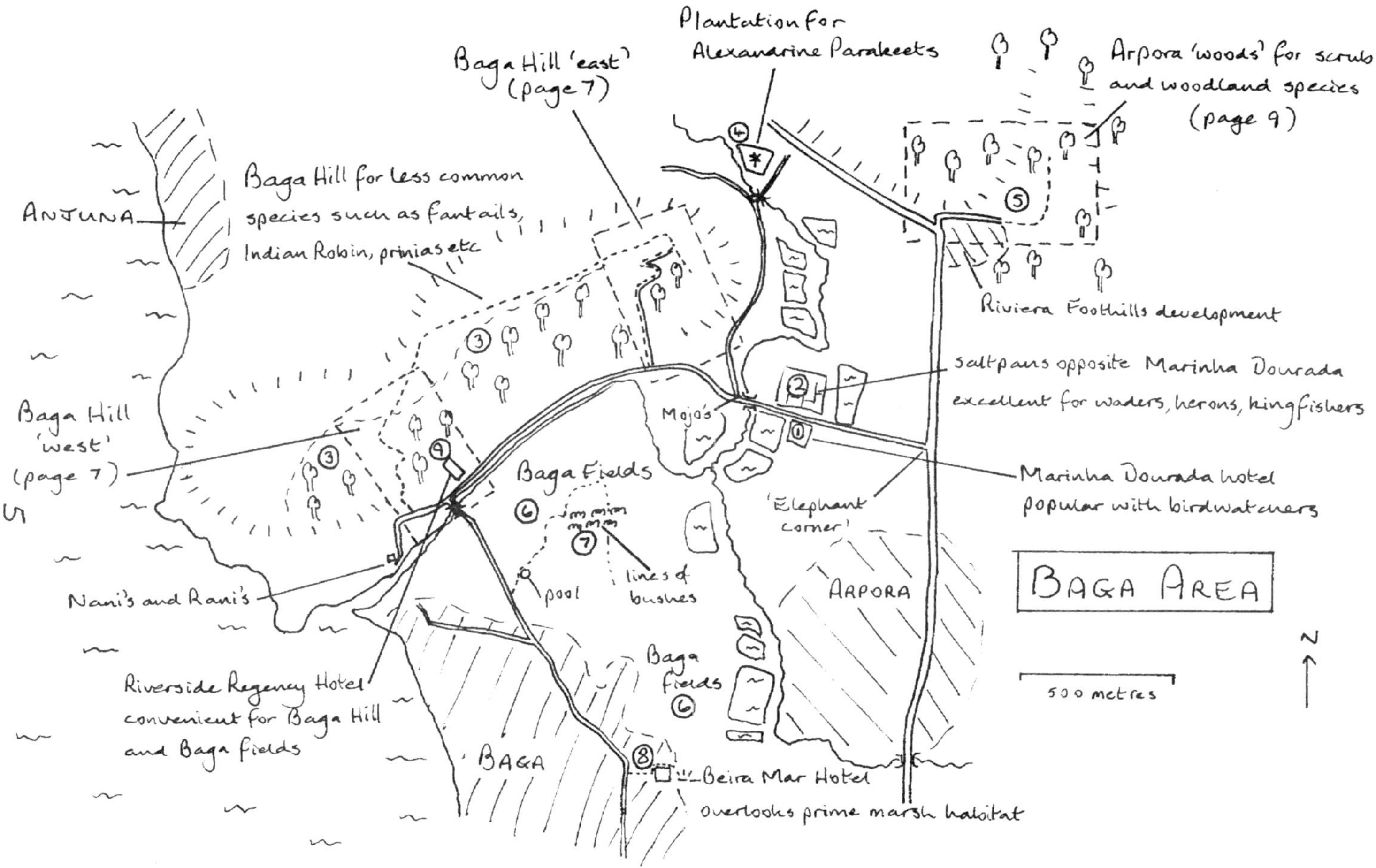
Plantation for
Alexandrine Parakeets
Baga Hill 'east'
(page 7)
Arpora 'woods' for scrub
and woodland species
(page 9)
ANJUNA
Baga Hill for less common
species such as fantails,
Indian Robin, prinias etc
Riviera Foothills development
saltpans opposite Marinha Dourada
excellent for waders, herons, kingfishers
Mojo's
Baga Hill
'west'
(page 7)
Baga Fields
Marinha Dourada hotel
popular with birdwatchers
'Elephant
corner'
pool
lines of
bushes
Nani's and Rani's
ARPORA
BAGA AREA
N
Baga
fields
500 metres
Riverside Regency Hotel
convenient for Baga Hill
and Baga fields
BAGA
Beira Mar Hotel
overlooks prime marsh habitat

Baga Hill

Attraction

Within easy walking distance of both the Marinha Dourada and the Riverside Regency, yet providing a chance to see a good variety of scrub and woodland species including Red Spurfowl, Indian Robin, Puff-throated Babbler and, in some years, Indian Pitta.

Getting there

There are two routes up the hill. One is found by walking west from Baga bridge looking for a track (15.5645N, 73.7493E) to the right immediately after the Montemar II apartment complex. Walk up the edge of this establishment then continue up some steps keeping a green fence on your right. Follow this to the top of the hill, birding en route. The other route is via a new tarmac road (15.5696N, 73.7562E) up the east end of the hill. Where the tarmac ends, a track to the left leads onto the plateau. You can walk the length of the plateau and connect with the other track, thus making an attractive round walk. Follow the best path you can find until, after passing through a couple of spots where the bushes close in, you'll see an overgrown path into the woodland on the left, next to a slab of bare rock (15.5677N, 73.7478E - see photos on www.findingbirds.co.uk).

Notes

1. It's possible to walk this part of the path and see very few birds but with patience I've seen White-throated Fantail, Orange-headed Thrush, Tickell's Blue Flycatcher, Thick-billed Flowerpecker, White-browed Bulbul, Black-headed Oriole, Small Minivet, Puff-throated Babbler and Brown-cheeked Fulvetta here. Indian Pitta has been seen here. I've had several sightings of Crimson Sunbird in bushes around the Montemar and once had 2 Vernal Hanging Parrots near Nani's and Rani's.

2. By walking the plateau area you stand a chance of seeing tricky species such as Red Spurfowl and Common Peafowl and this is a good site for Indian Robin (easily missed elsewhere). You'll see lots of drongos and bulbuls (including, possibly, Grey-headed) and there's a chance of prinias (typically Plain and Ashy), babblers (especially Jungle) and pipits (usually Paddyfield and Richards). Check the ever-present kites for White-bellied Sea Eagle, Booted Eagle and Oriental Honey Buzzard. I've also had Peregrine, Amur Falcon and Spotted Eagle over this hill and others have reported Steppe, Tawny, Changeable Hawk, Crested Serpent, Indian Spotted, Black and Bonelli's Eagles and Crested Goshawk though I can't guarantee they were all identified correctly.

3. The tarmac lane up to the east end of Baga Hill gives you a chance to look for birds at the edge of the forest including Jungle Babbler, Bronzed Drongo, Large-billed Crow, Alexandrine Parakeet, Black-lored Tit, Loten's Sunbird, Brown-cheeked Fulvetta, Grey-headed Bulbul and White-throated Fantail. As you reach the plateau, approach carefully, looking for peafowl in the grasses and Indian Robin in the first bushes by the barbed wire fence. I once had a party of Tawny-bellied Babblers along the 'loop-track'.

   Other birds reported at Baga Hill include: Banded Bay Cuckoo, Rufous Woodpecker, Yellow-crowned Woodpecker, Emerald Dove, White-browed Fantail, Grey-breasted Prinia and Black-faced Malkoha. Even rarer species reported have included Grey-necked Bunting (Mark Easterbrook), Indian Bushlark (Ray Thorneycroft), Nilgiri Wood Pigeon (Paul Wetton) and Little Spiderhunter.

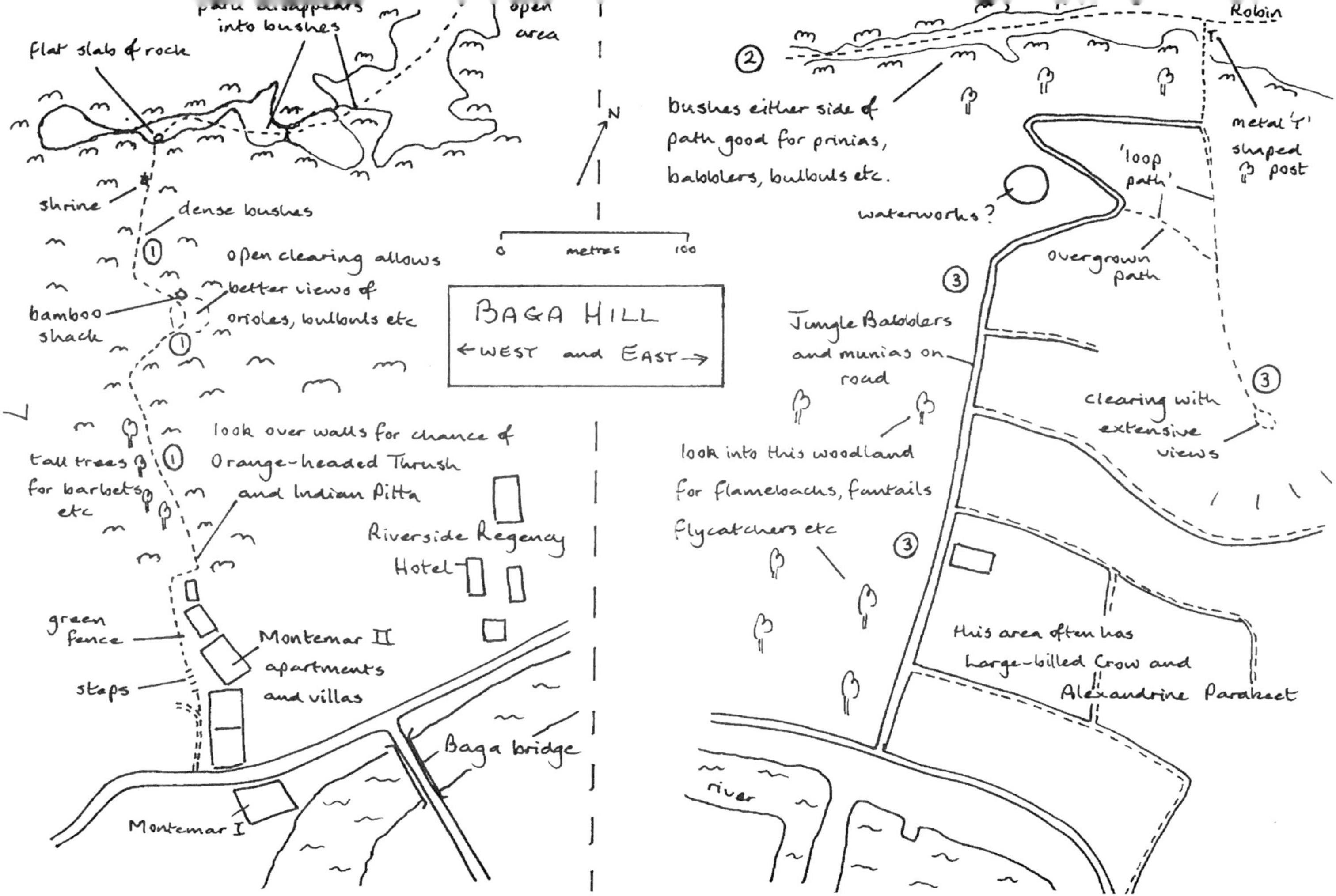
BAGA HILL
←WEST and EAST→
0 metres 100
N
Flat slab of rock
into bushes
open area
shrine
dense bushes
1
open clearing allows better views of orioles, bulbuls etc
bamboo shack
1
look over walls for chance of Orange-headed Thrush and Indian Pitta
1
tall trees for barbets etc
Riverside Regency Hotel
green fence
Montemar II apartments and villas
steps
Baga bridge
Montemar I
2
bushes either side of path good for prinias, babblers, bulbuls etc.
Robin
metal 'T' shaped post
'loop path'
waterworks?
overgrown path
3
Jungle Babblers and munias on road
3
clearing with extensive views
look into this woodland for flamebacks, fantails flycatchers etc
3
this area often has Large-billed Crow and Alexandrine Parakeet
river

Arpora Woods

Attraction

An easy walk from the Marinha Dourada, yet offering even wilder habitat than Baga Hill with a much longer species list. Some of the best, but most difficult, species to look for include Indian Pitta, Blue-faced Malkoha, Rufous Woodpecker and Yellow-crowned Woodpecker.

Getting there

From the Marinha Dourada, walk right to the junction with the main Anjuna road ('Elephant Corner'), then follow this north for about 800 hundred metres until the road bends to the left. At this point a small road goes to the right (15.5745N, 73.7651E), around the outer edge of the new 'Riviera Foothills' development. Follow this track beyond the entrance to Club Cubana and keep going. From anywhere else, just ask a taxi driver to take you to the Club Cubana or the Riviera Foothills.

Notes

1. In some years, Indian Pitta has been seen regularly along the track between the two walls, just past the club.

2. Immediately after the end of the wall on your right, take the track down the edge of the wall as far as a stream bed (15.5741N, 73.7681E). Although this is usually dry, it is a regular haunt of Nilgiri Blackbird, Orange-headed Thrush and Puff-throated Babbler. Indian Pitta has also been seen here.

3. The open area around this fork in the paths (15.5749N, 73.7685E) is good for birds such as sunbirds (including Loten's), flowerpeckers, bulbuls, drongos, orioles, barbets and munias. I've also had Jungle Babbler, Rufous Treepie, White-throated Fantail and Ashy Prinia and it was here that I saw a Blue-faced Malkoha in 2008.

4. The smaller track to the right leads to a more open area of fields and bushes where Loten's Sunbird, White-bellied Drongo, Common Woodshrike and Black-headed Cuckoo Shrike are regularly seen. Looking back to the main path from these fields you'll see a bare tree silhouetted on the skyline with a large nest in it. In some years, including 2009, this is occupied by a pair of White-bellied Eagles which regularly fly back and forth to the sea via Baga Hill.

5. The main track to the left passes a small quarry which is said to be the best spot for looking for the Blue-faced Malkoha. Other species I've had along this path include Grey-headed Bulbul and Bronzed Drongo.

6. When the track passes the second set of blue fence posts it reaches a small area of tall trees with a closed canopy (15.5773N, 73.7691E). This is the place to look for Rufous and Yellow-crowned Woodpeckers but they have been more elusive in recent years.

   Other species reported from here in various trip reports include: Mountain Imperial Pigeon, Indian Robin, Grey-breasted Prinia, Greater Flameback, Crimson Sunbird, Little Spiderhunter, Tawny-bellied and Dark-fronted Babbler, Bar-winged Flycatcher Shrike, Large Cuckoo-shrike, Jerdon's and Grey Nightjar and Oriental Scops Owl.

Arpora 'Woods'

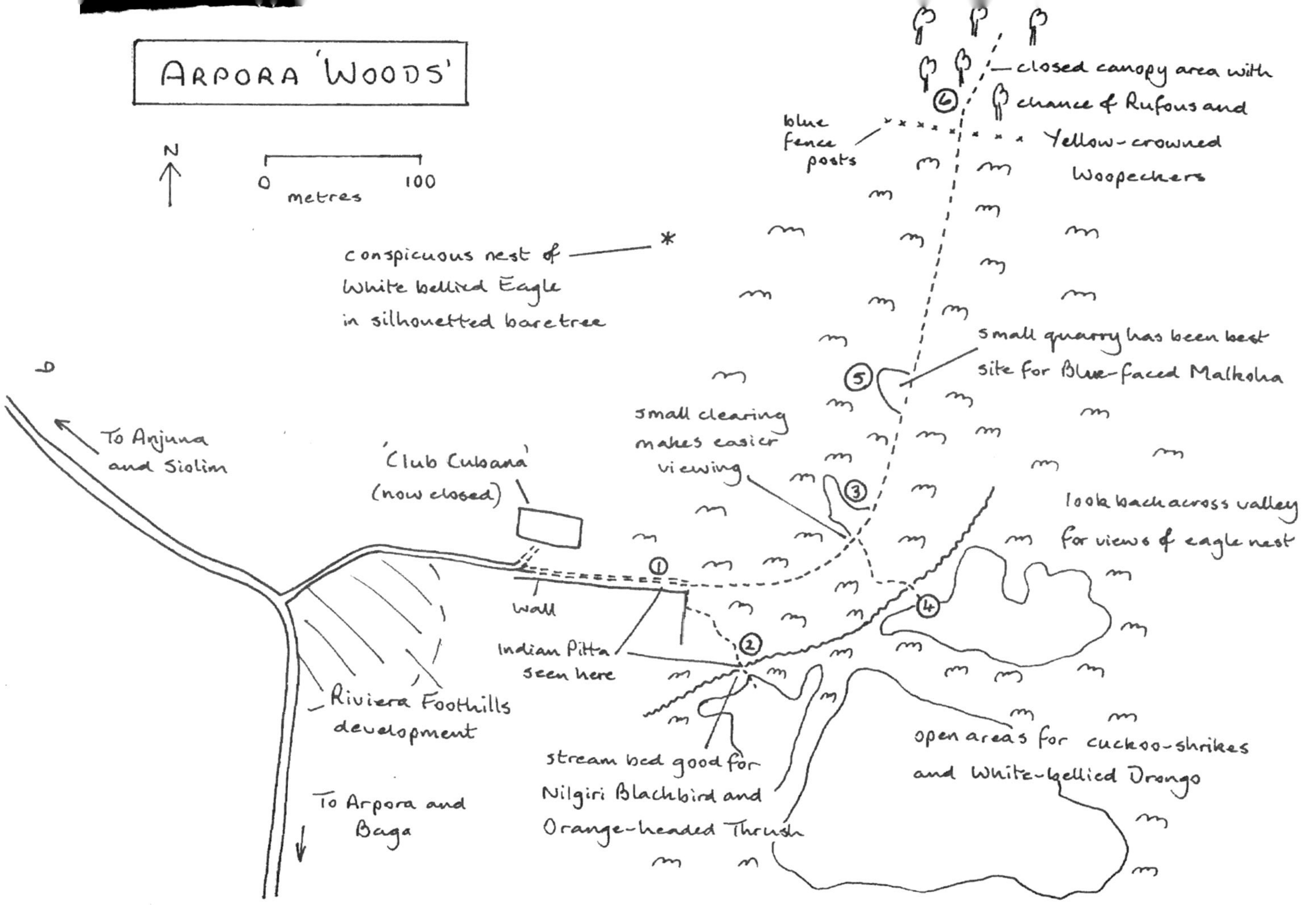

South of Calangute – Salgao and Pilerne

Attraction

The following sites are within an easy drive of Baga. Saligao Zor has lush woodland, famous for its roosting Brown Wood Owls. Pilerne Lake has Yellow-wattled Lapwings and in wet years a good selection of waterbirds. Fort Aguada has an infamous site for Indian Pitta.

Getting there

Saligao Zor is known to most taxi drivers, at least around Baga. Pilerne Lake is reached by turning south where the Calangute-Panjim road crosses a plateau. The turning is marked by an old temple on open ground. Follow this road down into a valley and park as soon as the lake comes into view.

Notes

1. Saligao Zor is a prominent hill above the village of Saligao. The road up the hill ends at a spring where a bathing pool has been built (15.5338N, 73.7865E). The pool is surrounded by lush vegetation and trees which continue around the top of the hill. The famous Brown Wood Owls usually roost close to the path just beyond the pool, where I've also had Asian Paradise Flycatcher, Red Spurfowl, Plain Prinia, Brown-cheeked Fulvetta, White-thoated Fantail and Rufous Woodpecker. By walking back down the lane you'll find a track to the right which goes behind the tall house and down to the stream below the pool. This area has had Malabar Whistling Thrush and even Oriental Dwarf Kingfisher; we had Puff-throated Babbler, Black-naped Monarch and more fulvettas and fantails. Other species reported from Saligao Zor have included Blue-faced Malkoha, Pompadour Pigeon, Indian Robin, Little Spiderhunter, Brown-headed Barbet, Jungle Prinia, Grey-breasted Prinia, Blue-capped Rock Thrush and Indian Pitta. By following the path to the top of the hill you reach a vantage point from which several species of eagle have been reported (Greater Spotted, Indian Spotted, Tawny and Steppe) as well as Amur Falcon.

2. From the pull-in at the north-east corner of the lake (15.5355N, 73.8152E), scan the fields and low walls for Yellow-wattled Lapwings amongst the commoner Red-wattled Lapwings. The wet fields between the road and the lapwings look promising for crakes, bitterns and painted-snipe. The lake itself varies in nature, depending on water levels. In 2009 when they were high, we had numerous Bronze-winged Jacanas, White-breasted Waterhen and Lesser Whistling Duck plus 3 Cotton Pygmy-goose. In 2008 there was barely any water in the lake; none of the above waterbirds were present but there was a spectacular gathering of Black and Brahminy Kites swooping for fish concentrated in a small pool at the west end of the lake (viewed from a second vantage point further along the road). In 2002, a wet year, R. Pritchard also had Pin-tailed Jacana, Painted Snipe and Blue-cheeked Kingfisher here.

3. There's also a small pool by the church at Candolim (15.5167N, 73.7771E). This is worth checking for waterbirds: in 2009 it had a Yellow Bittern that was easy to see for several days.

4. There are many sites where Indian Pittas have been seen in Goa but many of them change from year to year. A few taxi drivers such as Santosh Redkar will check a number of them to find a reliable one somewhere close to the coastal strip but, if you can't get hold of Santosh and you don't get to hear of another good site you may have to resort to looking for 'the Pitta in the Shitta'. This is a site close to Fort Aguada which has been reliable in the past but birders try to avoid it because, to get good views, you have to crouch in an area that is popularly used as the local toilet. If you HAVE to go there, park on the road outside the Taj Village Resort and find the path which goes east before the last of several cafe's (15.4988N, 73.7715E). Follow this path for 120 metres until you see a path to the right leading up to the next road. The ditch is on either side of that path (approx 15.4985N, 73.7728E). Other species reported by those who braved the elements have included Slaty-breasted Rail, Ruddy-breasted Crake, Tickell's Thrush, Nilgiri Blackbird and Sykes Warbler.

Saligao church
Saligao crossroads
main road to Mapusa
CALANGUTE
turn west before road bends left
temple
turn left just before temple on brow of hill
PILERNE LAKE
turn off to Calangute
wet fields have regular Spotted Eagle
SALIGAO ZOR pool and woodland for Brown Wood Owl etc
scan from here for Yellow-wattled Lapwing Jacanas, wildfowl etc.
open area on top of hill for raptors etc
view south end of lake from here
Candolim church
CANDOLIM
pool worth checking - has had Yellow Bittern
SOUTH OF CALANGUTE
N
0 km 1
ditch here is infamous site for Indian Pitta
FORT AGUADA
PANJIM

Morjim beach and Siolim rice fields

Attraction

The mouth of the Chapora river is the best place in Goa to see estuarine gulls, terns and waders and these are best viewed from the north (Morjim) side of the river. Nearby there is also a good site for the otherwise elusive Bay-backed Shrike and Brahminy Starling. Siolim rice fields can be superb as a wetland area for herons, storks, kingfishers, waders, jacanas and waterfowl.

Getting there

There is now a road across the river at Siolim. To reach Morjim, turn left once you have crossed the bridge and keep left, following the edge of the river until the road bends to the right and ends at a car park and some souvenir stalls (15.6184N, 73.7336E). This site is sometimes known as Turtle Beach. To reach the rice fields turn east at Siolim church and continue for almost 2 km looking for a turn to the left opposite Janessa's Beauty Salon (15.6159N, 73.7858E). This leads to the causeway with wetlands on both sides of the road.

Notes

1. Immediately behind the souvenir stalls are some sandy hollows where rubbish is thrown. This area is very popular with mynas and starlings, amongst which you should find some attractive Brahminy Starlings. Look carefully in the bushes around here as there is usually a Bay-backed Shrike present too. By walking around the sandy hollows between here and the hotels just inland, you stand a good chance of flushing Barred Button Quail. Other species reported here include Indian Silverbill and Red Avadavat.

2. By striking out south from the beach shacks of Turtle Beach (or from a pull-in at 15.6165N, 73.7354E) you will reach the mouth of the river. A few hours either side of high tide there will be sandbanks exposed at the tip and these are likely to be covered with flocking gulls and terns. You must first work out how to separate Brown-headed and Black-headed Gulls, then pick out other species such as Great Black-headed Gull, Slender-billed Gull, Crested Tern, Lesser Crested Tern, Gull-billed Tern, Heuglin's Gull and Steppe Gull (*barabensis*). Roseate Tern has also been reported here.

3. The rest of the beach usually has a number of waders so you can have fun sorting out Kentish Plover, Lesser Sandplover and Greater Sandplover. Small Pratincoles are regularly seen. The sandplovers seem to roost in the low vegetation just inland from the beach. Other species to have been reported here include Great Knot, Caspian Plover, Crab Plover and Grey-headed Lapwing.

4. When these rice fields are flooded they can be fantastic for birds, perhaps even as good as Carambolim Lake. In November 2009 there were hundreds of egrets, herons, sandpipers, Little Cormorants and Lesser Whistling Duck, 4 species of kingfisher, at least 80 Open-billed Stork and small numbers of both Bronze-winged and Pin-tailed Jacanas. The distant areas to the east are often good for flocks of Small Pratincoles and there have been several sightings of Grey-headed Lapwing here.

5. (not illustrated) En route to here there is a good site for Yellow-wattled Lapwing. On the road from Arpora to Siolim, after passing the roundabout with a turn-off to Anjuna, look in the fields to the right (15.5938N, 73.7721E) before the building bearing an advert for the Goan Beach Club.

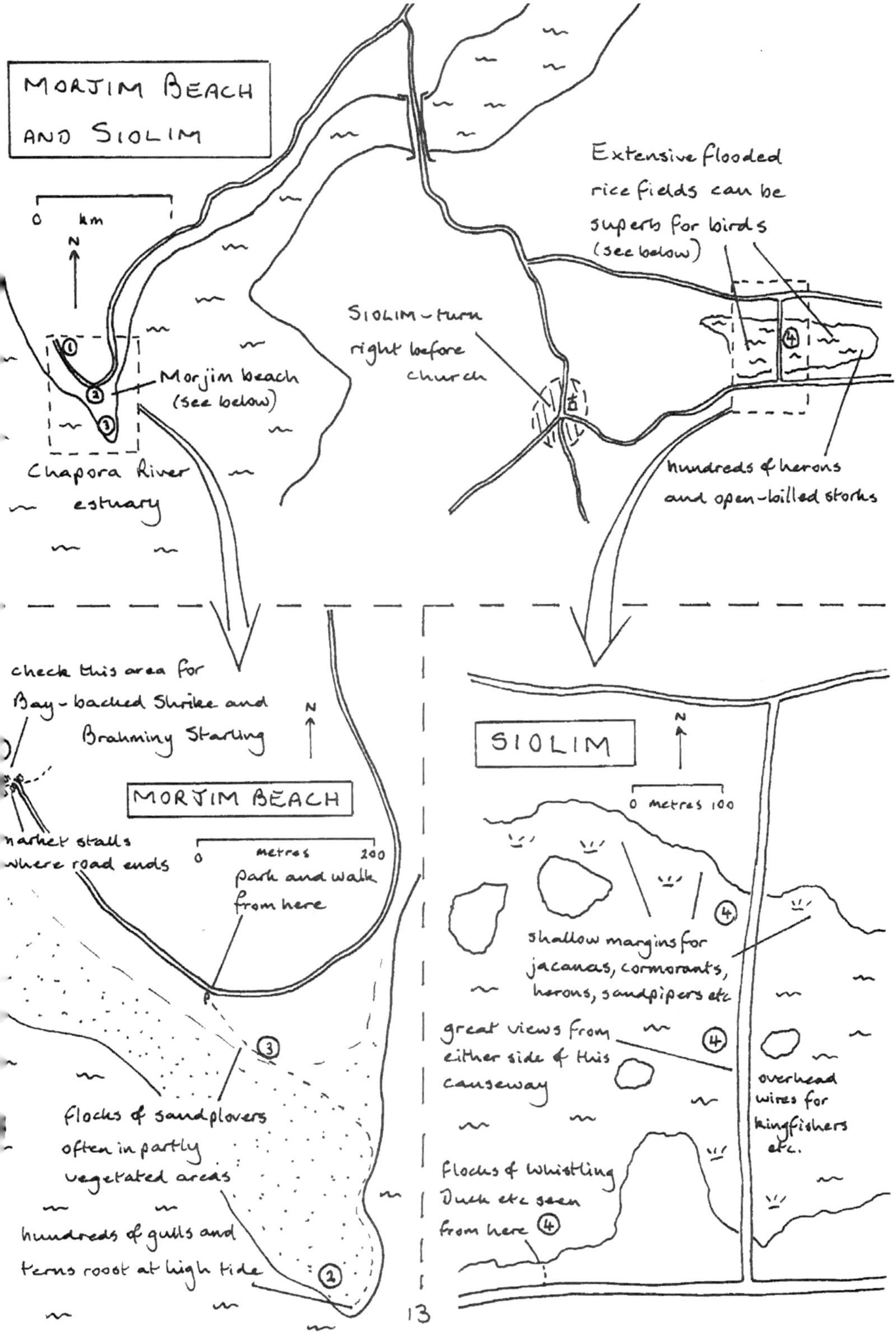

MORJIM BEACH AND SIOLIM
0 km
N
Morjim beach (see below)
Chapora River estuary
SIOLIM - turn right before church
Extensive flooded rice fields can be superb for birds (see below)
hundreds of herons and open-billed storks
check this area for Bay-backed Shrike and Brahminy Starling
N
MORJIM BEACH
0 metres 200
market stalls where road ends
park and walk from here
flocks of sandplovers often in partly vegetated areas
hundreds of gulls and terns roost at high tide
SIOLIM
N
0 metres 100
shallow margins for jacanas, cormorants, herons, sandpipers etc
great views from either side of this causeway
overhead wires for kingfishers etc.
flocks of Whistling Duck etc seen from here

Dona Paula

Attraction

An open raised plateau area that is being developed but, so far, still has the main target birds: Ashy-crowned Sparrow-lark and Yellow-wattled Lapwing. Other species to look for include Oriental Skylark Isabelline Wheatear and Indian Robin.

Getting there

Dona Paula is well signposted on the road that goes west from Panjim. The best sites are along the road to the east of the roundabout in Dona Paula, as shown.

Notes

1. One site is along a new road (15.2596N 73.81517E) between the main road and a prominent radio tower. The rough ground here has lots of Oriental Skylark (which sing like Skylarks but have a striking 'bazz' call) and you should soon locate Ashy-crowned Sparrow-lark too. Tawny Pipit and Yellow-wattled Lapwing are often seen here and I've also had Short-toed Lark, Malabar Lark, Isabelline Wheatear, Indian Robin, Paddyfield and Richard's Pipits and numerous Hoopoes.

2. If the first site fails to turn up Yellow-wattled Lapwing, try the open ground (15.4584N, 73.8189E) on the other side of the road, before the International Centre.

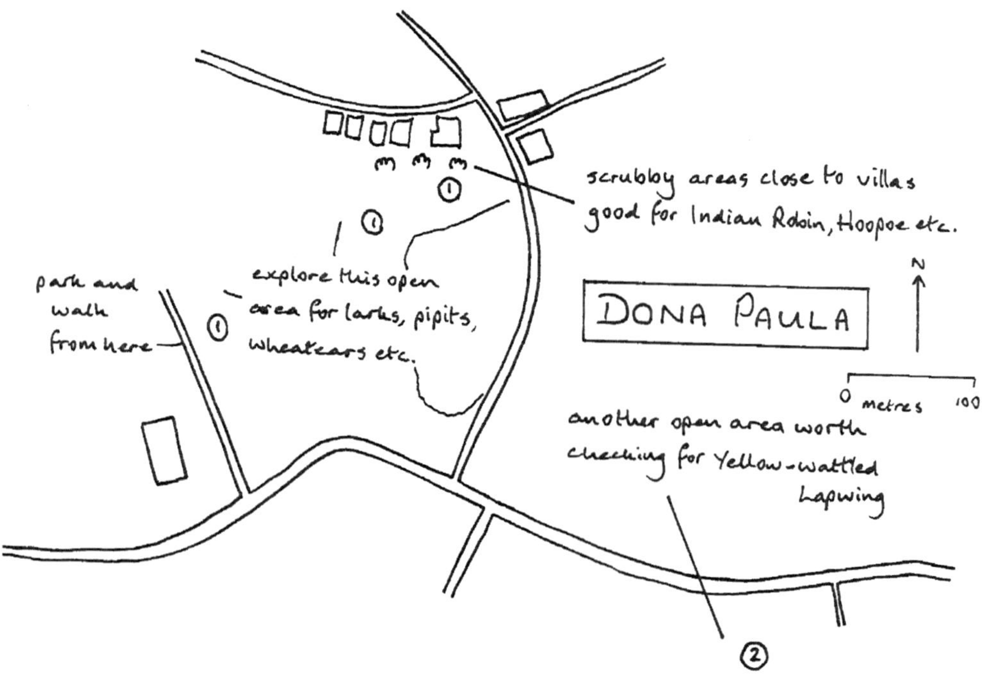

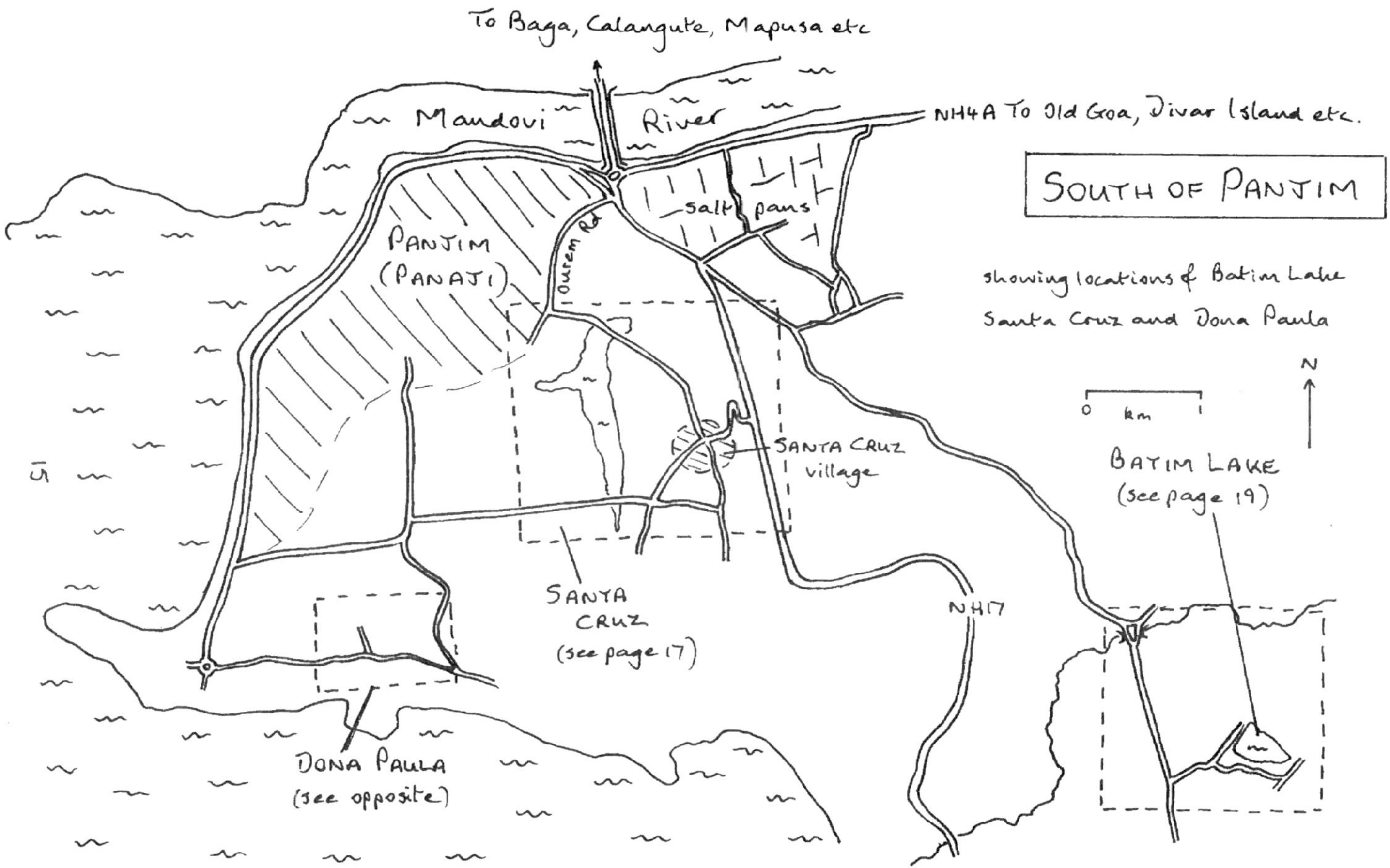
South of Panjim
To Baga, Calangute, Mapusa etc
Mandovi River
NH4A To Old Goa, Divar Island etc.
showing locations of Batim Lake
Santa Cruz and Dona Paula
N
0 km
salt pans
Ourem Rd
Panjim
(Panaji)
Santa Cruz village
Batim Lake
(see page 19)
Santa Cruz
(see page 17)
NH17
Dona Paula
(see opposite)

Santa Cruz

Attraction

An area with several wetland habitats including saltpans, paddyfields an estuarine creek and a lake. Good birds here in 2008 included Paddyfield Warbler, Great Spotted Eagle, Woolly-necked Stork, Indian Cormorant, Terek Sandpiper and Small Pratincole. It is said to be a good site for Citrine Wagtail and Cinnamon Bittern.

Getting there

Santa Cruz village is about 3 km south of Panjim or you may reach here by driving east from Dona Paula (page 14)

Notes

1. Take the path to the north (from 15.4712N, 73.8393E), parallel with the tidal channel. From here you can view the tidal marsh to the left and the paddyfields to the right. The bushes on the edge of the tidal marsh had Ashy Prinia, Plain Prinia, Zitting Cisticola and Paddyfield Warbler. In 2009 the paddyfields had interesting groups of waders, mostly common species such as stints, ringed plovers and redshanks but also 20 Small Pratincoles. In the drier year of 2008, however, the best birds we had were Pintail Snipe, a flock of Baya Weavers and several Plum-headed Parakeets taking nest material into the palm trees. A Great Spotted Eagle scanned over the tidal creek from one of the palms.

2. A path to the left (from 15.4776N, 73.8393E) takes you across the tidal creek. From here you can get views of more waterbirds including some Indian Cormorants (Little Cormorants too). The wet fields to the north of this path had a gathering of Woolly-necked Storks and Spoonbills.

3. The road between Santa Cruz and Panjim passes more tidal pools and saltpans. The tidal pools (15.4858N, 73.8378E) opposite a large shrine with a red roof had a collection of estuarine waders including Terek Sandpiper, Dunlin, Ruff and Pacific Golden Plover. The saltpans (15.4875N, 73.8341E) had fewer birds but these included a flock of about 40 Small Pratincole.

4. Due east of Santa Cruz village there is a lake(15.4773N, 73.8504E) just the other side of a crossroads on the eastern side of the main Panjim/Margao road. In the past it has had waterbirds such as lesser Whistling Duck and both species of Jacana but it is becoming more overgrown and therefore difficult to view from the road.

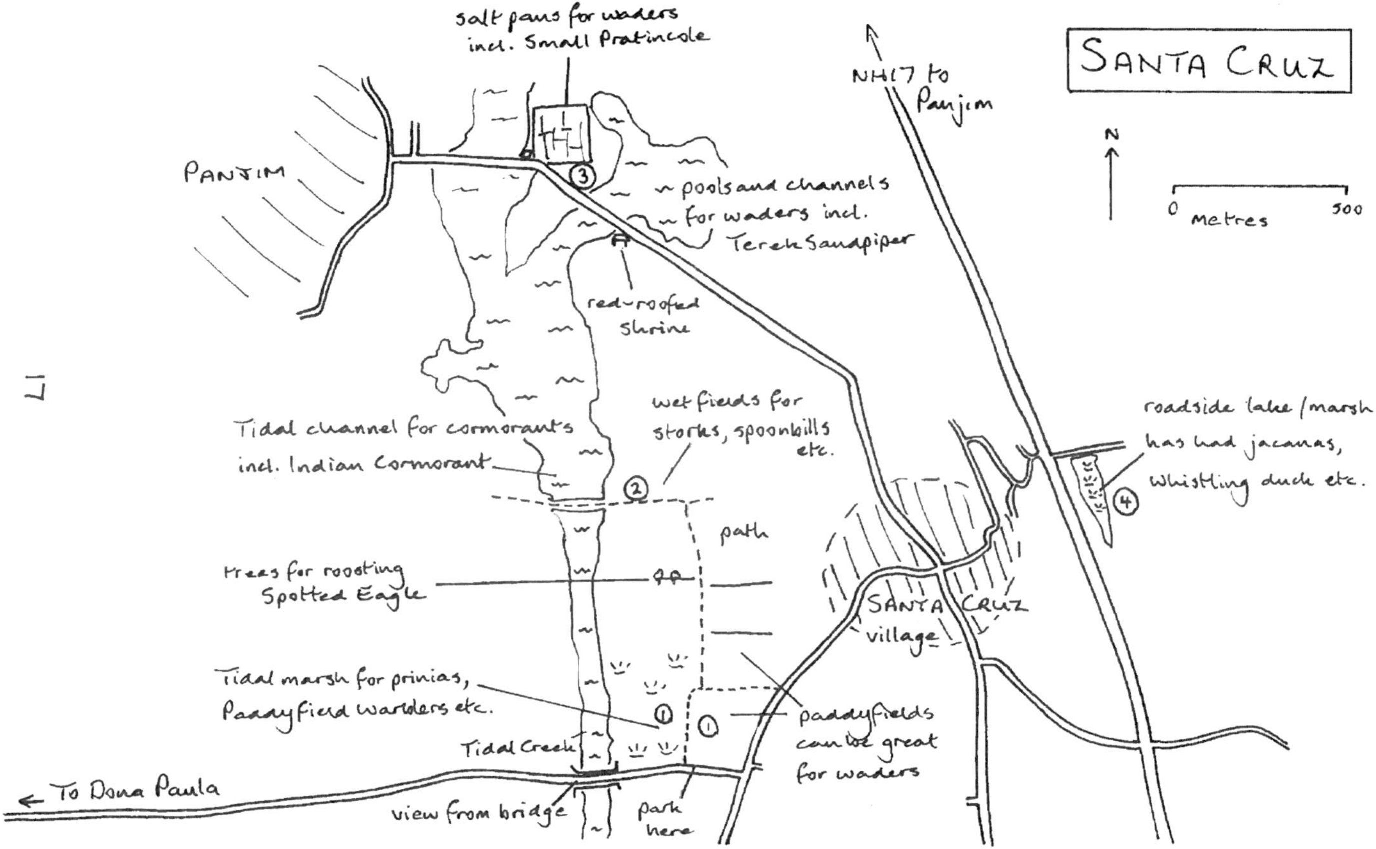
SANTA CRUZ
N
0 metres 500
NH17 to Panjim
salt pans for waders incl. Small Pratincole
3
pools and channels for waders incl. Terek Sandpiper
PANJIM
red-roofed shrine
wet fields for storks, spoonbills etc.
Tidal channel for cormorants incl. Indian Cormorant
2
path
trees for roosting Spotted Eagle
SANTA CRUZ village
roadside lake / marsh has had jacanas, whistling duck etc.
4
Tidal marsh for prinias, Paddyfield warblers etc.
1
1
paddyfields can be great for waders
Tidal Creek
To Dona Paula
view from bridge
park here

Batim Lake

Attraction

In dry seasons, most of the waterbirds such as ducks and jacanas concentrate at a few sites such as Carambolim and are unlikely to be found at places such as Pilerne and Siolim. However, in 2008, Carambolim was also dry so the best remaining site for these species was Batim Lake. In fact, since this lake is smaller, it is easier to work and may actually provide better views than at Carambolim. You can expect Lesser Whistling Duck, Cotton Pygmy-goose, Purple Swamphen and both jacanas here; Comb Duck, Spot-billed Duck and Darter are also possible and the nearby saltpans can be good for waders.

Getting there

From Panjim, a main road goes south-east through Merces then drops down to a river plain. The saltpans are just after the bridge and the lake is found by turning left at Batim Youth Club (15.4478N, 73.8843E).

Notes

1. Saltpans vary in productivity according to water levels but on my first visit here there were plenty of waders, mostly common European stuff but including Marsh Sandpipers and Temminck's Stints. They could be viewed by parking near the cafe at 15.4576N, 73.8813E.

2. The road from the Youth Club passes the west end of the lake but, although many birds are visible from here (especially Purple Swamphen and Lesser Whistling Duck), the light is awful in the morning since the lake is to the east. Even so, I also saw Cotton Pygmy-goose from here in 2009.

3. Turn east at the big white chapel and park where the road forks (next to a hollow often full of Pond Herons - 15.4477N, 73.8903E). Walk to the lake from there; creep up behind the lakeside bushes to get the best views possible. From here we saw thousands of ducks, mostly Lesser Whistling Duck and Garganey but also lots of Shoveler, Pintail and Teal. Careful scanning yielded a few pairs of Cotton Pygmy-goose and Bronze-winged Jacana, 3 Comb Duck, 2 Spot-billed Duck, a Darter and 4 species of Kingfisher.

4. Keep left along the lanes and you'll reach the east side of the lake. There's less open water here but it's perfect for lots of Purple Swamphen and Bronze-winged Jacana. There was a flock of about 30 Pheasant-tailed Jacanas, mostly a little further out, but I got close to them by walking around the building at the NE corner (15.4508N, 73.8939E). There were more Cotton Pygmy-goose here and a pair of Crested Serpent Eagle to the east.

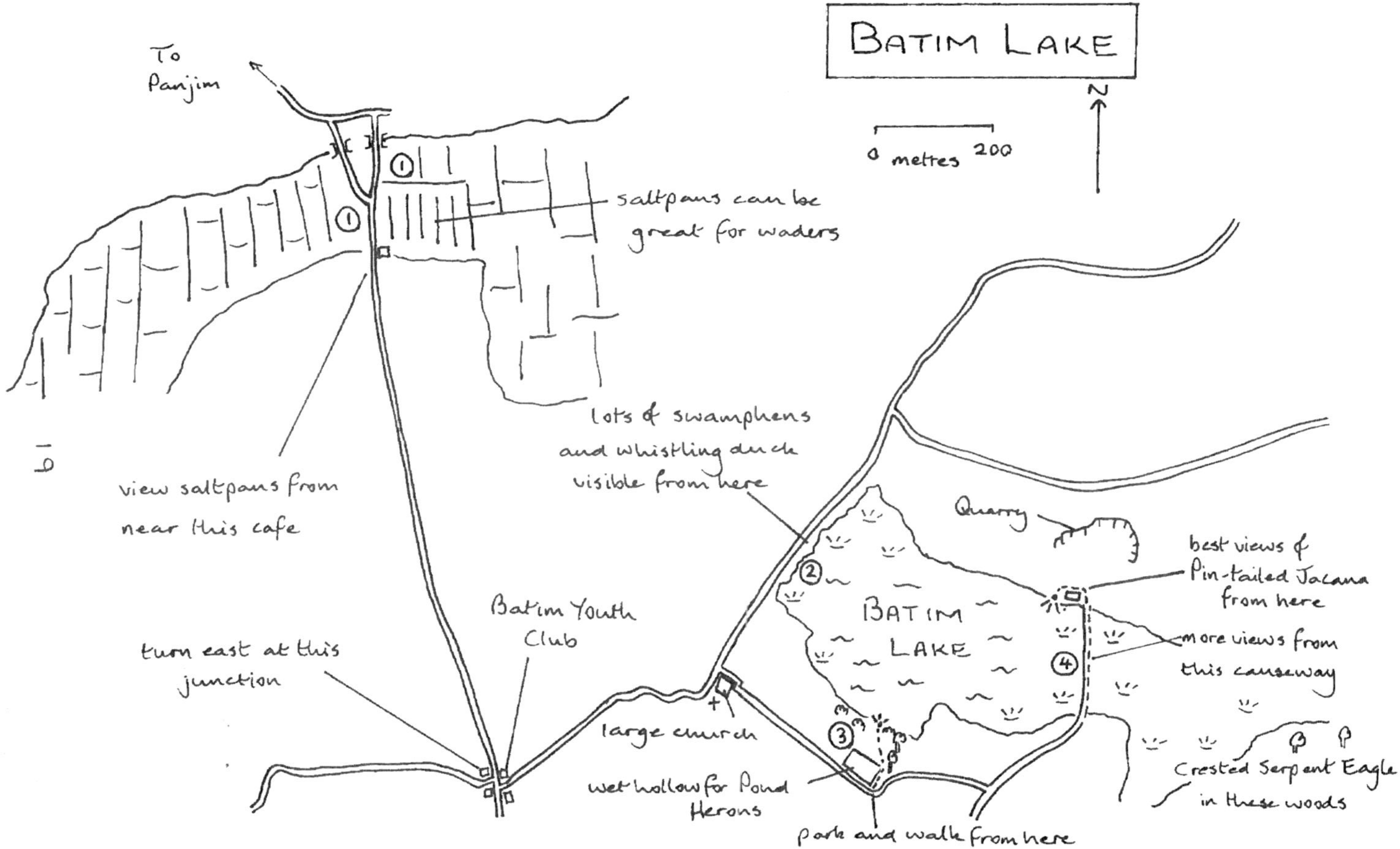
BATIM LAKE
N
0 metres 200
To Panjim
1
1
saltpans can be great for waders
view saltpans from near this cafe
lots of swamphens and whistling duck visible from here
turn east at this junction
Batim Youth Club
large church
wet hollow for Pond Herons
park and walk from here
2
3
4
BATIM LAKE
Quarry
best views of Pin-tailed Jacana from here
more views from this causeway
Crested Serpent Eagle in these woods

Chorao and Divar islands

Attraction

There is a large nature reserve (Salim Ali Bird Sanctuary) on Chorao Island on the north side of the river which has mangroves with breeding herons and storks. Nearby Divar island has many waterbirds but is most popular for its regular evening passage of harriers flying to roost.

Getting there

Both islands can be reached by ferry from Ribandar (to Chorao) or Old Goa (to Divar). The ferry leaves Old Goa from the jetty at 15.5004N, 73.8776E.

Notes

1. As you arrive by ferry on Chorao island, there are some 'scrape-like' fields to the right which Harris described as 'the best wader site in Goa'. However, Chorao island is no longer one of the most popular trips for visiting birders, who generally prefer instead to scan from a distance (see 2 and 3 below).

2. Park near the Ribandar junction (15.5038N, 73.8623E) and scan the far mangroves for birds of Chorao Island such as Lesser Adjutant Stork and the closer sandbars for birds such as Gull-billed Tern and Terek Sandpiper. At high tide the waders may instead be on the saltpans to the south of the road. These can be accessed via a number of small pull-ins (eg 15.5012N, 73.8482E)

3. Another site overlooking Chorao island is on the north side of the river, just upstream from the main bridge. Scan from the churchyard at Britona (15.5093N, 73.8432E).

4. The road across Divar Island passes lots of pools and mangroves which might be worth exploring. I've had Purple Heron, Ashy Prinia and Clamorous Warbler.

5. A long, straight stretch of road passes an area of open fields including a football pitch. Along here is a lone tree (15.5153N, 73.8908E). Park there and explore the fields. In this area I've had Spotted Little Owl, Oriental Skylark, flocks of Short-toed Lark, Paddyfield Pipit, Richard's Pipit, Little Ringed Plover, Siberian Stonechat, Woolly-necked Stork, Rain Quail and a Pied (Jacobin) Cuckoo. Harriers are regularly in view, especially in the evening when birds pass here on the way to roost going roughly NE to SW. Marsh, Montagu's and Pallid Harriers are all likely. Lesser Florican has been seen in these fields too and Rufous-tailed Lark is seen regularly in some years.

Chorao and Divar Islands

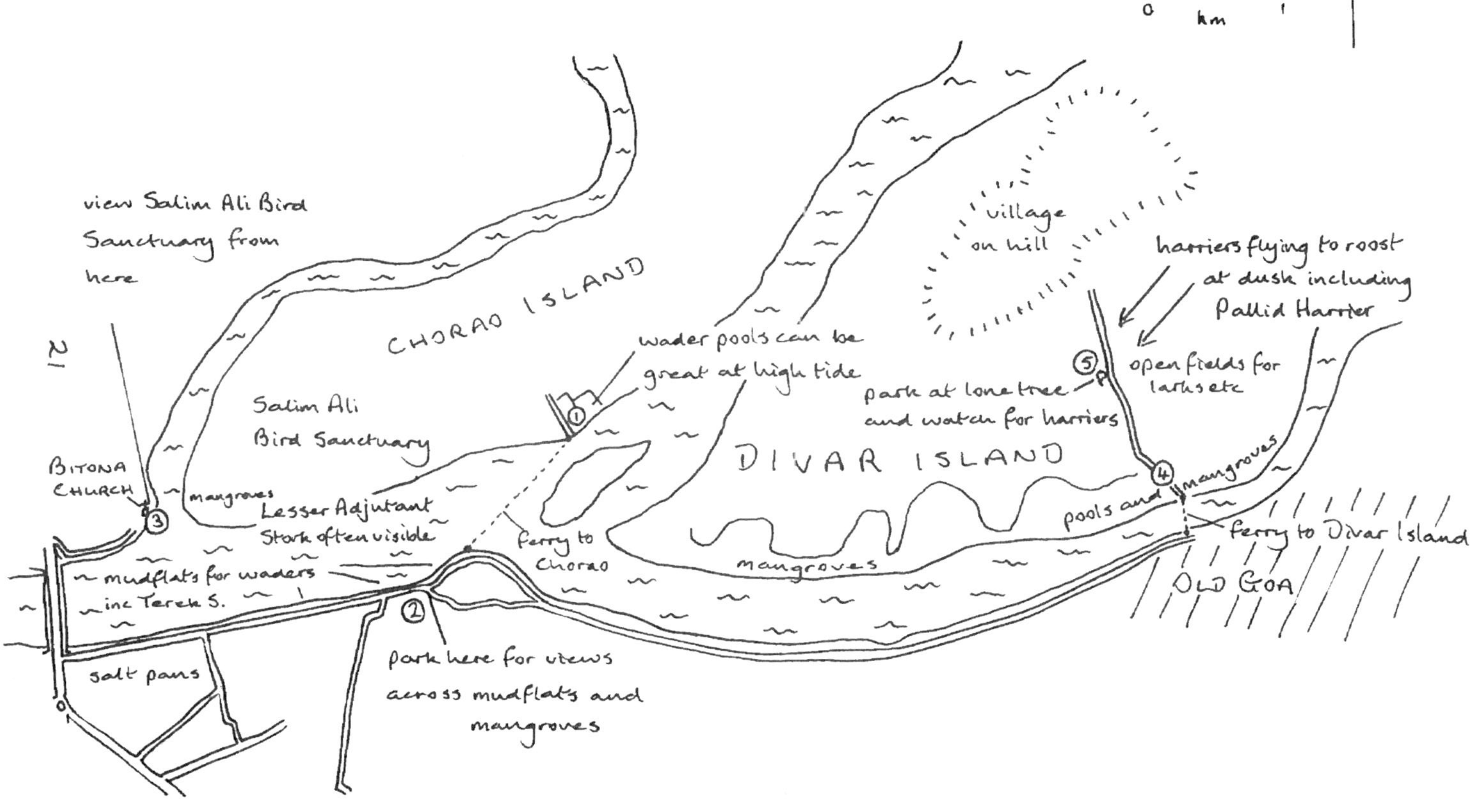

Mayem (or Maem) Lake

Attraction

The lake itself has relatively few waterbirds but the surrounding woods have many good birds. Specialities include Orange-breasted Green Pigeon, Nilgiri Wood Pigeon, nesting Crested Serpent Eagle and two Grey Nightjars that sit all day close to the path. There is no longer a reliable, accessible roosting site for Brown Fish Owl here and past reports of roosting Indian Nightjar were apparently erroneous.

Getting there

There is a lakeside resort at Mayem, so it is well-known to most taxi-drivers. Coming from Bicholim you pass the lake on your left then take the first turning 15.5747N, 73.9390E) to the 'Mayem Lake View bar and restaurant'. Park and walk alongside the lake from there. Even in the dry year of 2008 the water level was too high to allow a complete circuit of the lake.

Notes

1. By scanning over the lake from near the car park you can get distant views of birds in the far trees including Orange-breasted Green Pigeon, Malabar Grey Hornbill and Greater Racket-tailed Drongo. We also heard Indian Scimitar Babbler, Red Spurfowl, Grey-headed Bulbul and Little Spiderhunter. You should also see 4 species of kingfisher and other waterbirds such as Little Cormorant and White-breasted Waterhen. Birds over the lake included Crested Treeswift

2. The walk down the west side of the lake passes through open woodland in which you'll see birds such as Ashy, Bronzed and White-bellied Drongo, Drongo Cuckoo, Black-headed Cuckoo-shrike, Common Wood-shrike, Blue-capped Rock Thrush, Verditer Flycatcher, Asian Paradise Flycatcher, Rufous Treepie, Greater Coucal, Purple and Purple-rumped Sunbirds, Vernal Hanging Parrot, flowerpeckers, iora, barbets, bulbuls etc

3. The pond at the far end of the lake looks perfect for Brown Fish Owl but there's no longer a stake-out for them here. However, there are two very obliging Grey Nightjars which sit on branches within sight of the path and a pair of Crested Serpent Eagle that are regularly seen and heard overhead. The area on the far side of the pond is a reliable site for Malabar Whistling Thrush, Nilgiri Blackbird and Puff-throated Babblers. In 2009 we managed to get reasonable views of both Indian Scimitar Babbler and Little Spiderhunter close to the path. Other species I've seen around the pool include Chestnut-headed Bee-eater, Nilgiri Wood Pigeon, Racket-tailed Drongo and Grey-headed Bulbul.

   Other birds reported at Mayem lake include Rufous Woodpecker, Yellow-crowned Woodpecker, Changeable Hawk Eagle (has nested, giving excellent views), Emerald Dove, Crimson Sunbird and Yellow-footed Green Pigeon.

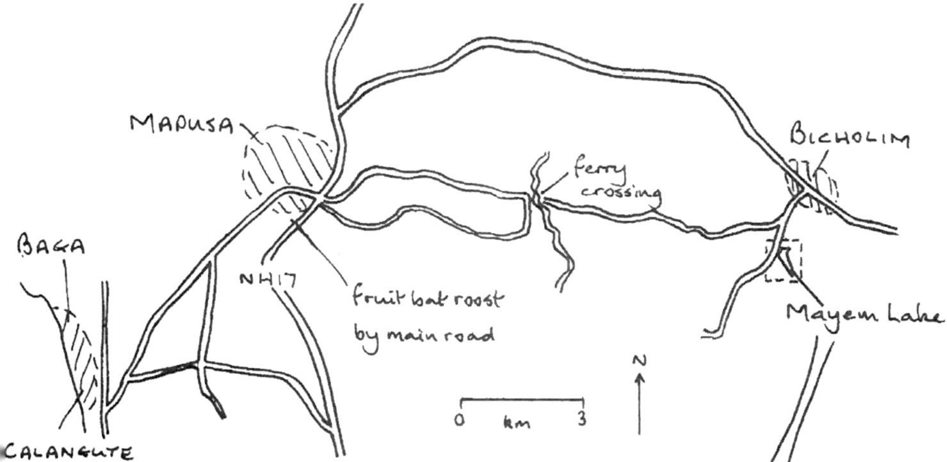
MAPUSA
BAGA
CALANGUTE
NH17
fruit bat roost by main road
ferry crossing
BICHOLIM
Mayem Lake
N
0 km 3

MAYEM LAKE

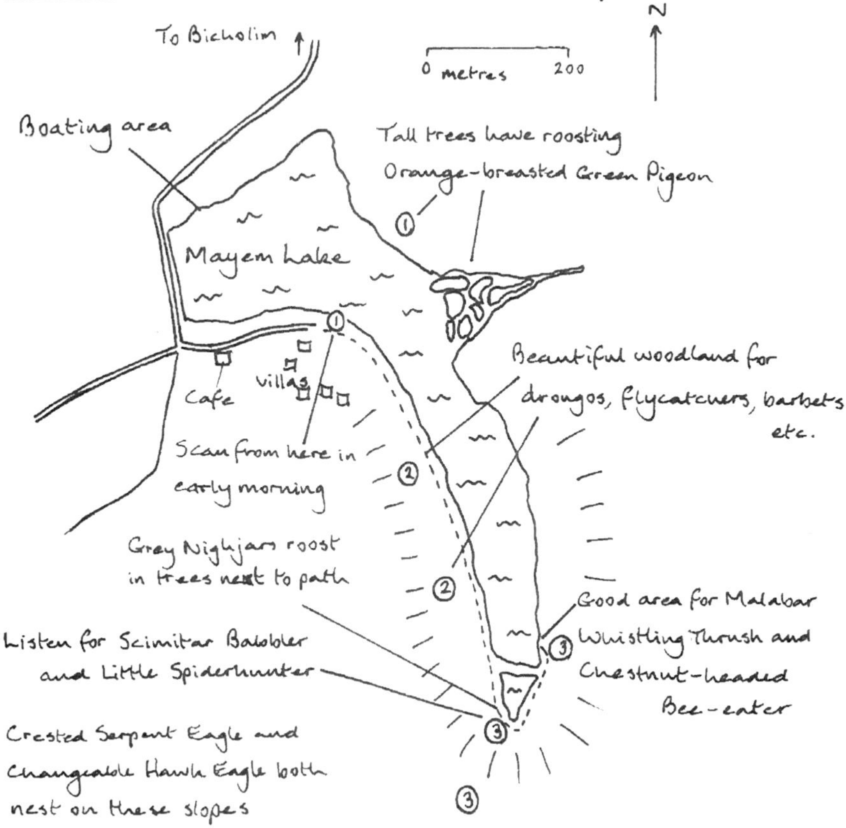
To Bicholim
N
0 metres 200
Boating area
Tall trees have roosting Orange-breasted Green Pigeon
Mayem Lake
Cafe
Villas
Scan from here in early morning
Beautiful woodland for drongos, flycatchers, barbets etc.
Grey Nighjars roost in trees next to path
Good area for Malabar Whistling Thrush and Chestnut-headed Bee-eater
Listen for Scimitar Babbler and Little Spiderhunter
Crested Serpent Eagle and Changeable Hawk Eagle both nest on these slopes

Carambolim Lake and Wood

Attraction

Carambolim Lake seems to have recovered from the period in 2007-08 when it was drained and had very few birds. Once again you can expect thousands of birds here including Lesser Whistling Duck, Cotton Pygmy-goose and both species of Jacana. The area is also worth visiting for the nearby wood which is a known stake-out for Jungle Owlet and Brown Hawk Owl.

Getting there

As you approach Old Goa, there is a major junction at which the 'by-pass' bends right towards Ponda. At this point, there is a sharper right turn which leads past Karmali Railway station to the road at the south of the lake. The best route for the wood is to take the by-pass and, after crossing the railway line, take the next signposted right turn (15.4965N, 73.9309E - opposite the Gokulam bar). From there, keep left whenever the road forks (ignoring sharper turns to the left) until you drop down a slope and see the wood at the end of a straight road.

Notes

1. If the lake is full, you will have hundreds, maybe thousands, of birds, including Lesser Whistling Duck, Purple Swamphen, Little Cormorants and Bronze-winged Jacanas and smaller numbers of Cotton Pygmy-goose, Darters and Pheasant-tailed Jacanas all of which should be visible from the track along the south of the lake. Look out for Gull-billed and Whiskered Terns and birds flying over such as Osprey, Booted eagle, Black-headed Ibis, Open-billed and Lesser Adjutant Storks. The pipe (15.4861N, 73.9300E) across the south-east corner of the lake makes a great perching place for kingfishers – I've had 4 species here.

2. The paddyfields to the south of the lake can also be excellent for birds. This is often where Open-billed Storks and Lesser Adjutants rest and up to 1000 Small Pratincoles have occurred. Other species reported from here have included Terek Sandpiper, Long-toed Stint, Baer's Pochard and Citrine Wagtail.

3. Unless the tracks are exceptionally wet, it should be possible to drive to the observation towers on the east side of the lake (eg. 15.4927N 73.9306E). These provide more views of the sort of birds visible from the causeway but in a much quieter environment. The mature woods/gardens opposite the most northerly tower are worth checking – we had Rufous Woodpecker and Jungle Owlet in 2009. The large trees in the north-west corner often have a Spotted Eagle sitting in them.

4. The wood (15.4825N, 73.9413E) has a family of Spotted Owlet (around the first disused building), a pair of Brown Hawk Owl (roosting high in the palms above the path to the building on the south side of the road) and a pair of Jungle Owlet (high in the trees towards the east side of the wood). The wood is also good for bulbuls, coucals, flowerpeckers, flamebacks, orioles, barbets, sunbirds etc. From the edges of the wood, check the bushes and wires for Black-shouldered Kite, Spotted Eagle, Rosy Starling and Baya Weavers. Red Collared Dove was reported here in 2002.

5. Beyond the wood is an area of marshland that can be good for waders (eg 40 Terek Sandpiper in 2002), herons and cormorants and the distant bushes often have Spotted Eagle and Lesser Adjutant. This area can be viewed from the back of the wood (15.4805N, 73.9435E).

CARAMBOLIM LAKE AND WOOD

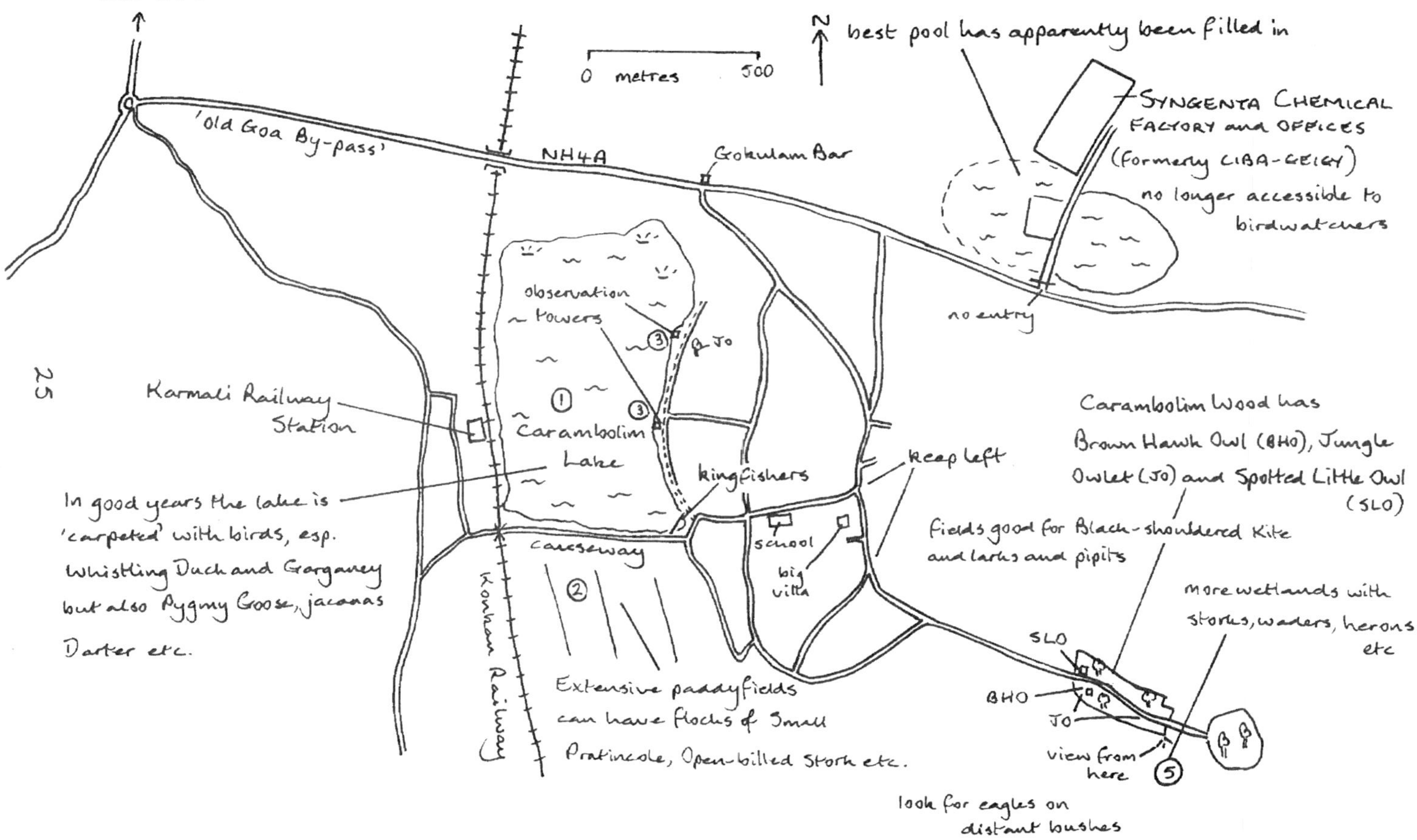

Zuari river trip

Attraction

The best way to look for two otherwise difficult kingfishers – Black-capped and Collared – is to take a boat trip up the river Zuari with Kamat, a boatman who knows the birds well and is practised in getting you close to them. You should see 4 other species of kingfisher too and Kamat will try to show you other species such as storks, herons and eagles sitting in the riverside trees. Altogether a thoroughly enjoyable experience.

Getting there

The boat sails from a small jetty (15.4083N, 73.9084E), immediately east of the Konkan bridge on the south side of the river. To get there, cross the river heading south then double back sharply left at the first roundabout (15.4026N, 73.9080E), following signs to Ponda. In 2009 the boat trip cost 1000 rupees each (not counting the taxi to get you there).

Notes

1. The first destination will be the posts in the estuary to the west of the bridges. River Tern has been reported here but usually you just get great views of Crested Tern.

2. Kamat will take you up a couple of side creeks where he will spot the kingfishers for you, switch off the boat engine and glide up to the birds giving great views. On our 2009 trip we did the same thing with Spotted Eagle, Woolly-necked Stork, Black-headed Ibis, Striated Heron and Night Heron. Look out too for Gull-billed Terns over the river, Clamorous Reed Warblers in the mangroves and birds overhead – we had Lesser Adjutant Stork and Steppe Eagle.

3. The trip takes you almost as far upriver as Carambolim Wood. In that area, there used to be a loafing spot for a flock of Terek Sandpipers but this site has been lost due to the construction of a new dam. On the plus side, the area within that dam has become a regular site for Ruddy Shelducks – we saw about 40.

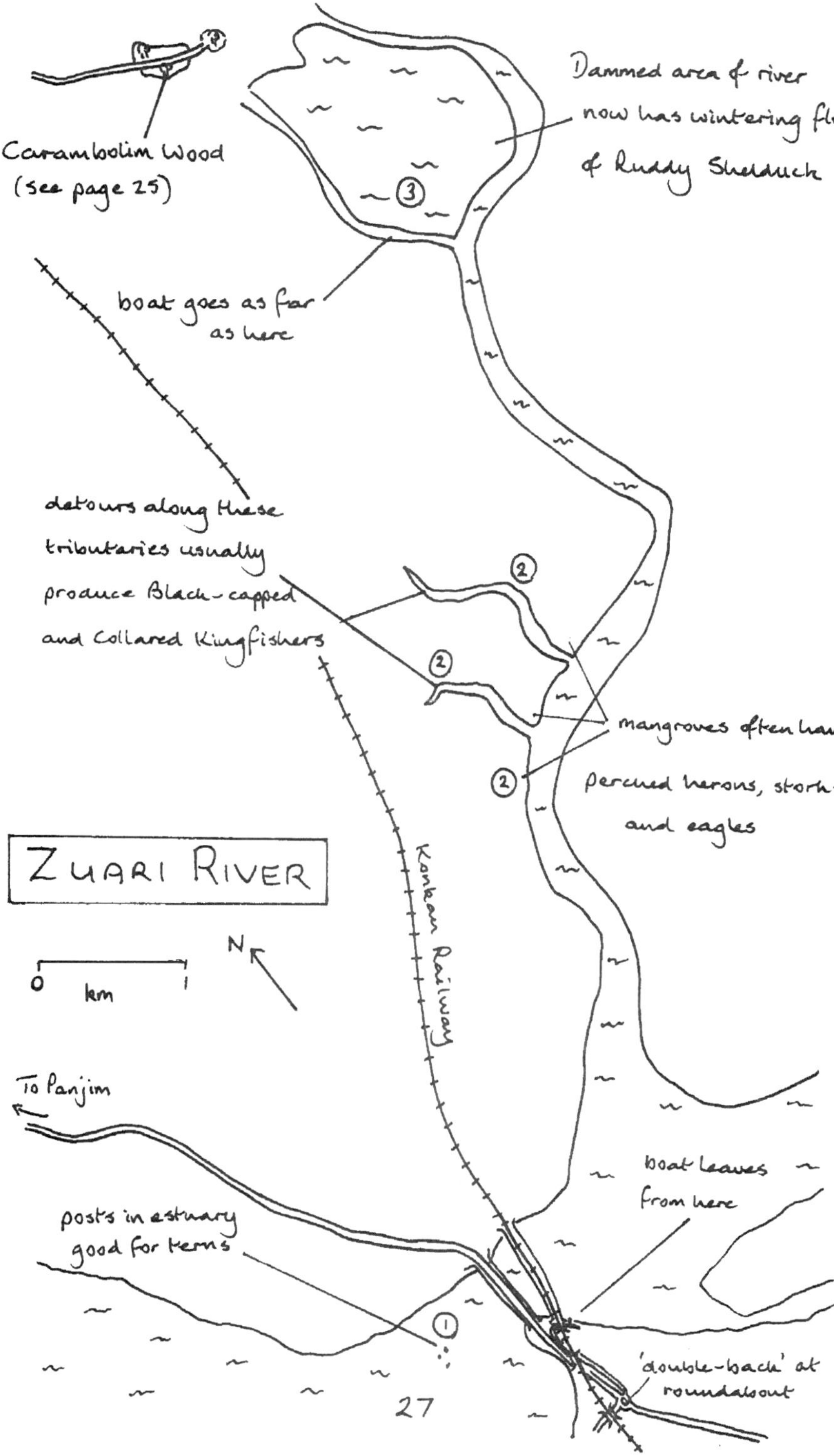
Carambolim Wood
(see page 25)
Dammed area of river
now has wintering flocks
of Ruddy Shelduck
3
boat goes as far
as here
detours along these
tributaries usually
produce Black-capped
and Collared Kingfishers
2
2
2
mangroves often have
perched herons, storks
and eagles
ZUARI RIVER
Konkan Railway
N
0
km
1
To Panjim
boat leaves
from here
posts in estuary
good for terns
1
'double-back' at
roundabout

Backwoods area - Bhagwan Mahaveer National Park

Attraction

The Bhagwan Mahaveer National Park has always been the best place to find most of the rarer, endemic and semi-endemic forest species in Goa but now it is possible to see them with the help of local experts by staying at the Backwoods camp on the road to the temple at Tamdi Surla. By staying at the camp you will have the opportunity to benefit from their expertise and spend the best parts of the day (dawn and dusk) birding in these superb areas. This will enable you to see the best species of the Park without needing to visit the various sites described by Harris, though no doubt these are also productive.

Access

The Backwoods staff will arrange for you to be picked up from your hotel on the coast and taken to the 'camp' (which has very comfortable tents and chalets), usually for a 2-night stay. (As you are picked up before dawn, this gives you almost 3 full days in the area; longer stays are also possible). During this time you will visit some of the following sites in small groups with a local guide and transport provided. Further details are given at www.**backwoodsgoa**.com or you can email them to book your places at backwoodsindia@hotmail.com

Notes

1. The camp itself (15.439N 74.234E) has many of the most exciting birds, including, potentially, Sri Lanka Frogmouth, Brown Fish Owl, Spot-bellied Eagle Owl, Malabar Trogon and Indian Pitta (see page 30).

2. Just before entering the Bhagwan Mahaveer park, you pass a village with an obvious school building (Barabhumi High School - 15.4307N, 74.1952E). The lanes around here are good for birds such as Vernal Hanging Parrot, Malabar (Crimson-fronted) Barbet (here alongside Coppersmith Barbet – their songs are confusingly similar), Malabar Pied Hornbill, Nilgiri (Plain) Flowerpecker, Blackheaded Cuckoo-shrike and Large Wood-shrike. The house opposite the school has some flowering bushes in the garden which attract a variety of sunbirds including Loten's and, occasionally Little Spiderhunter. From here we were treated to fly-past views of a Great Hornbill. Yellow-wattled Lapwing and Bar-winged Flycatcher-shrike have been seen here in the past.

3. This area of open ground, near a fabulously multi-coloured house (15.4410N, 74.2299E), is a great place for watching for raptors. On our visit in 2008, we saw Shikra, Besra, Crested Goshawk, Black-shouldered Kite, Oriental Honey-buzzard and White-eyed Buzzard but there's also a chance of eagles such as Black, Changeable Hawk, Mountain Hawk and Rufous-bellied. Other birds seen around the village included Chestnut-headed Bee-eater, Red Spurfowl, Malabar White-headed (Chestnut-tailed) Starling, Taiga Flycatcher, Crested Treeswift, Pompadour Pigeon, Crimson-fronted Barbet and flocks of munias (including Scaly-bellied and Black-headed) which, in 2009 included a few Red-headed and Black-headed Buntings.

4. The temple at Tamdi Surla is not only a popular tourist destination it's also a great spot to look for species such as Oriental Dwarf Kingfisher, Blue-cheeked Kingfisher, Blue-bearded Bee-eater, Malabar Trogon, White-bellied Woodpecker and Jerdon's Nightjar (see page 32).

Bhagwan Mahaveer – Backwoods Area

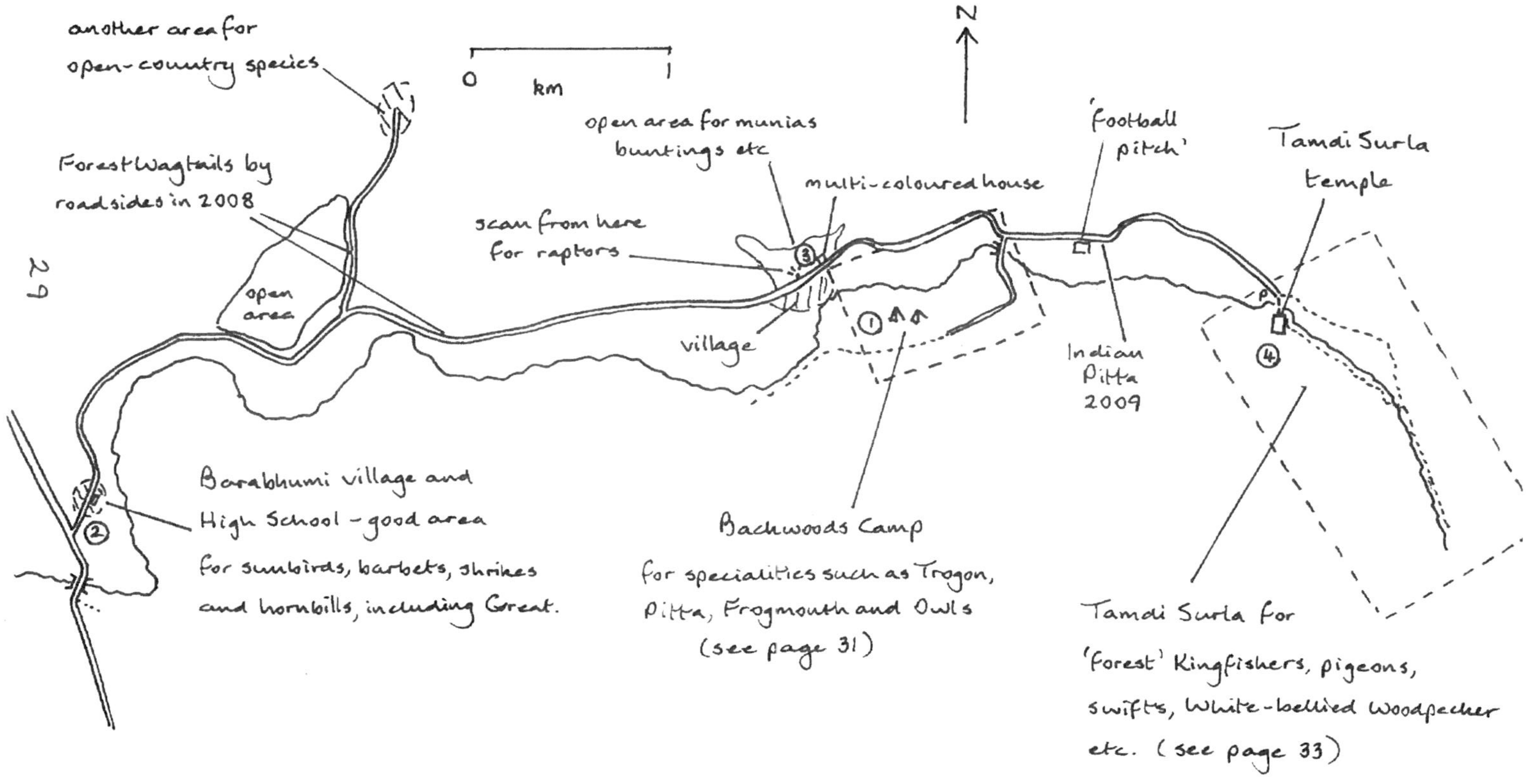

Backwoods camp

Attraction

The camp is set in a mixture of habitats including closed-canopy forest, open fields and a seasonal river. The staff will know which key species are viewable during your visit and will take you directly to birds such as owls, pittas and frogmouths if they are there.

Access

The camp itself is private, for paying guests only. The following notes should help you find birds around the camp during 'down-time'periods when you are free to wander around.

Notes

1. Birds seen by us around the junction with the Tamdi Surla road included Vernal Hanging Parrot, Pompadour Pigeon, Black Bulbul, Crested Serpent Eagle, Rufous-bellied Eagle, Streak-throated Swallow and Crested Tree Swift. In 2009 we also saw Blue-eared Kingfisher from the bridge.

2. Around the open fields and bare trees were species such as Peafowl, Red Spurfowl, Heart-spotted Woodpecker, Brown-capped Pygmy Woodpecker, Chestnut-shouldered Petronia, Brown Shrike, Spangled Drongo, Black-lored Tit and Malabar Parakeet.

3. The river which runs around the back of the camp regularly has Brown Fish Owl (chased off by Jungle Crows as we approached) and Forest Wagtail (though in both 2008 and 2009 this was scarce around camp). Blue-cheeked Kingfisher and Little Spiderhunter are also possible here.

4. In the woodland to the left of the track (as you walk into camp) I've had species such as Red Spurfowl, Malabar Trogon, White-rumped Shama, Fairy Bluebird, Western Crowned Warbler, Dark-fronted Babbler and Puff-throated Babbler. This is also the area where the Sri Lanka Frogmouth roosts but it's not worth looking for it without the help of a guide.

5. On my visits, birds seen in and around the camp itself have included Malabar Trogon, White-rumped Shama, Malabar Parakeet, Malabar Grey Hornbill, Common Hawk-cuckoo, Black-naped Oriole, Fairy Bluebird, Malabar Whistling Thrush, Shikra, Racket-tailed Drongo, Spangled Drongo, Scarlet Minivet, Forest Wagtail and Heart-spotted Woodpecker. There are a couple of pools close to the dining area and these attract birds such as Yellow-browed Bulbul, Flame-throated (=Black-crested) Bulbul, Orange-headed Thrush and Brown-cheeked Fulvetta, all giving fantastic views. The waste water from the kitchen runs off into a channel which attracts Nilgiri Blackbird and, occasionally, Indian Pitta, a species that is more regularly seen coming before dawn to a dripping tap within camp. A walk after dark is likely to produce owls: Brown Wood, Collared (Indian) Scops and, possibly, Oriental Scops. The guides can also show you Spot-bellied Eagle Owl in some years; apparently they breed every other year (they didn't in 2007-8 or 2009-10)

6. There are tracks into the woodland to the south of the camp. By following these with a guide in 2008 we managed to see Heart-spotted Woodpecker, Rufous Woodpecker, White-bellied Woodpecker, Racket-tailed Drongo, Malabar Parakeet, White-eyed Buzzard and lots of Western Crowned Warbler.

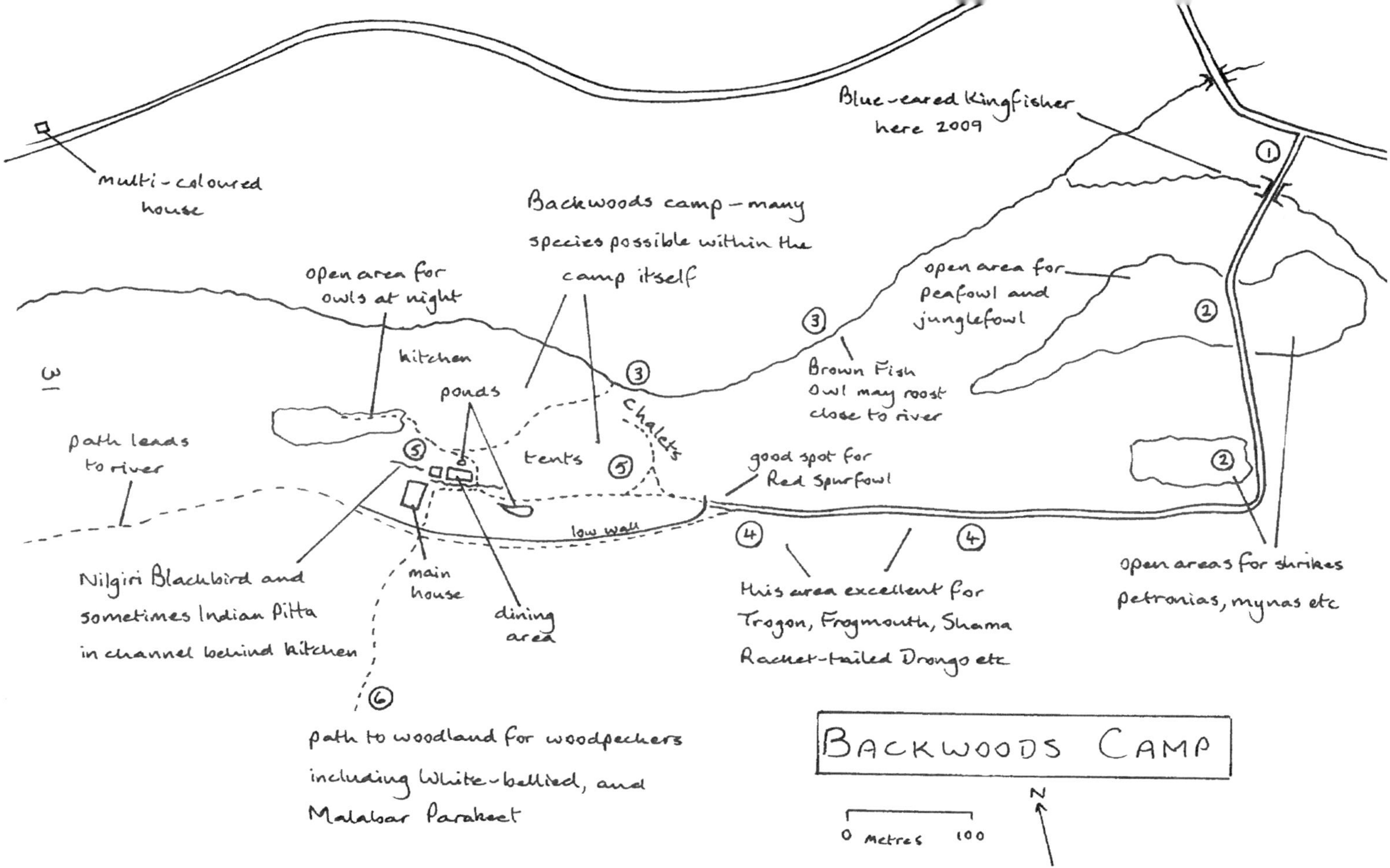
BACKWOODS CAMP
Blue-eared Kingfisher here 2009
multi-coloured house
Backwoods camp – many species possible within the camp itself
open area for owls at night
kitchen
ponds
tents
Chalets
open area for peafowl and junglefowl
Brown Fish Owl may roost close to river
good spot for Red Spurfowl
low wall
path leads to river
Nilgiri Blackbird and sometimes Indian Pitta in channel behind kitchen
main house
dining area
This area excellent for Trogon, Frogmouth, Shama Racket-tailed Drongo etc
open areas for shrikes petronias, mynas etc
path to woodland for woodpeckers including White-bellied, and Malabar Parakeet
1
2
2
3
3
4
4
5
5
6
0 metres 100
N

Tamdi Surla

Attraction

The open area immediately around the temple will have a few interesting birds but the main attraction is the river, the surrounding woodland and the nearby fields where key species such as Oriental Dwarf Kingfisher, White-bellied Woodpecker and Jerdon's Nightjar are possible.

Getting there

This is a popular tourist destination. There may even be trips to here from the coastal resorts but, of course, you'd need to be here at dusk for the nightjars.

Notes

1. You should see your first kingfishers from the bridge next to the car park (15.4406N, 74.2519E), but probably (only) White-throated, Stork-billed and/or Common Kingfishers. It's a good spot for Brown-throated Flycatcher and Malabar Whistling Thrush too.

2. In the trees around the edge of the open temple area we had Malabar Pied Hornbill, Crimson-fronted Barbet, Oriental Honey-buzzard, Orange-headed Thrush and Blue-capped Rock Thrush. By scanning from here you should see Mountain Imperial Pigeon and possibly an eagle such as Black Eagle. There's also a good chance you will at least hear White-bellied Woodpecker.

3. To the far left of the temple (as you first see it) is a path alongside the river. If you approach here carefully you may be lucky enough to see an Oriental Dwarf Kingfisher but they are more likely to be seen further upstream. They are very elusive and likely to fly before most of the party get to see them. However, this is a good spot for Blue-eared Kingfisher too; we had great views of one about 500 metres or so upstream. Along these tracks I've also seen species such as Emerald Dove, Black-naped Monarch, White-bellied Blue Flycatcher, Velvet-fronted Nuthatch, Greater Flameback, Asian Paradise Flycatcher, Verditer Flycatcher and others in the party have had Blue-bearded Bee-eater and Large-billed Leaf Warbler. Extraordinarily we also found a flycatcher trapped in the guey web of one of those massive Wood Spiders – it proved to be a Blue-throated Flycatcher.

4. On the other side of the river are some open fields which are good for Jerdon's Nightjar at dusk and should be checked for Grey Junglefowl. In the woods around here, we also had White-bellied Woodpecker, Mountain Imperial Pigeon, Grey-fronted (Pompadour) Pigeon, Large Wood-shrike, Black Bulbul, Vernal Hanging Parrot and Malabar Trogon. It's worth scanning from this open area, not just for pigeons and raptors (we had Rufous-bellied Eagle) but also for swifts; we had Little Swift, White-rumped Needletail and Brown-backed Needletail.

   Other species reported from Tamdi Surla have included Great Hornbill, Indian Scimitar Babbler and Grey Nightjar

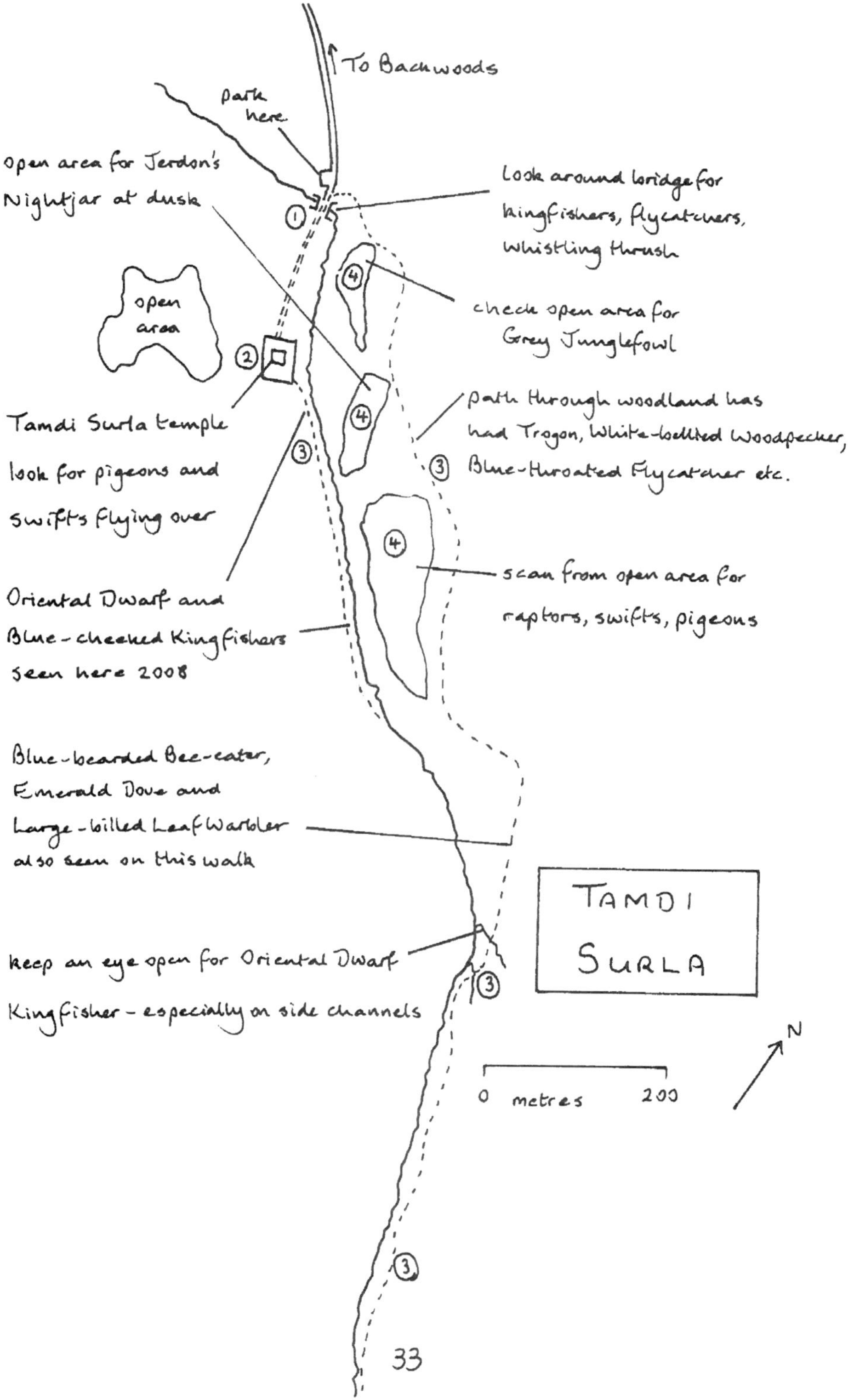
To Backwoods
park here
open area for Jerdon's Nightjar at dusk
Look around bridge for kingfishers, flycatchers, whistling thrush
1
4
check open area for Grey Junglefowl
open area
2
Tamdi Surla temple
look for pigeons and swifts flying over
path through woodland has had Trogon, White-bellied Woodpecker, Blue-throated Flycatcher etc.
3
4
3
4
scan from open area for raptors, swifts, pigeons
Oriental Dwarf and Blue-cheeked Kingfishers seen here 2008
Blue-bearded Bee-eater, Emerald Dove and Large-billed Leaf Warbler also seen on this walk
TAMDI SURLA
keep an eye open for Oriental Dwarf Kingfisher - especially on side channels
3
N
0 metres 200
3

Bondla

Attraction

One of three main forest sanctuaries in Goa, the others being Bhagwan Mahaveer (Molem) and Cotigao (in south Goa). As this one is the closest to the north Goan resorts it is the easiest to do in a day trip by taxi. Most of the Western Ghats forest species can be found here, including sought-after species such as Malabar Trogon, Little Spiderhunter, Grey Junglefowl, Brown Fish Owl, Oriental Scops Owl, Sri Lanka Frogmouth, Indian Pitta, Oriental Dwarf Kingfisher and Bar-winged Flycatcher-shrike.

Getting there

From Ponda, take the NH4A road towards Molem but turn north just after Tisk and continue for about 7 km until the River Mandovi appears on your left. Look for a right turn to Bondla Wildlife Sanctuary (Zoo) by the village of Gangem (15.4663N, 74.0892E). This is the so-called 'approach road' mentioned in many trip reports. It can be followed for about 4 km to the entrance to the zoo. Stop en route for good birding.

Notes

1. It pays to set off early from the coast to arrive on the approach road around dawn. 350 metres from the start of the road is a turning to the right across a bridge (15.463201° 74.089033°). This area is very productive and it is worth walking the next 600 metres to a spot (15.4585N, 74.0899E) where there are tracks on either side of the road. Both tracks are worth taking, especially the one to the west which leads to an open area where birds are more easily seen. In 2008, we quickly saw lots of species such as Malabar Whistling Thrush, Orange-headed Thrush, Red Spurfowl, Little Spiderhunter, Racket-tailed Drongo, Rufous Woodpecker, Malabar Grey Hornbill, Fairy Bluebird, Scarlet Minivet, Rufous Treepie, Besra, Brown-headed Barbet and no less than 6 species of bulbul, including Black Bulbul. In 2009 we saw similar species but also had great views of a Changeable Hawk Eagle.

2. Towards the end of the approach road it rises and has a few sharp bends. We explored that area and had species such as Malabar Trogon, Grey Junglefowl, Black-naped Monarch, Velvet-fronted Nuthatch, Western-crowned Warbler and had amazing views of a perched Besra. Even better, on our 2009 visit we had prolonged views of an Oriental Dwarf Kingfisher.

3. Near the top of the slope is a reservoir on the left. This has long been a stakeout for Brown Fish Owl but the roost wasn't occupied in 2008 or 2009. By exploring this area in 2009 we had White-rumped Shama, Fairy Bluebird, Grey Junglefowl, Malabar Whistling Thrush and Blue-capped Rock Thrush and Loven from Backwoods showed us a roosting site for 3 Oriental Scops Owls.

4. By turning sharp left by the entrance to the zoo you climb to another car park and a useful restaurant. You should see Spotted Deer feeding near the restaurant and we also had Blue-capped Rock Thrush and Greater Flameback.

5. Beyond the entrance to the zoo, the road continues down to a car park (15.4325N, 74.1098E). By walking this route we had birds such as Western-crowned Warbler, Velvet-fronted Nuthatch and Brown-capped Pygmy Woodpecker but the best bird was a Bar-winged Flycatcher-shrike. Species reported

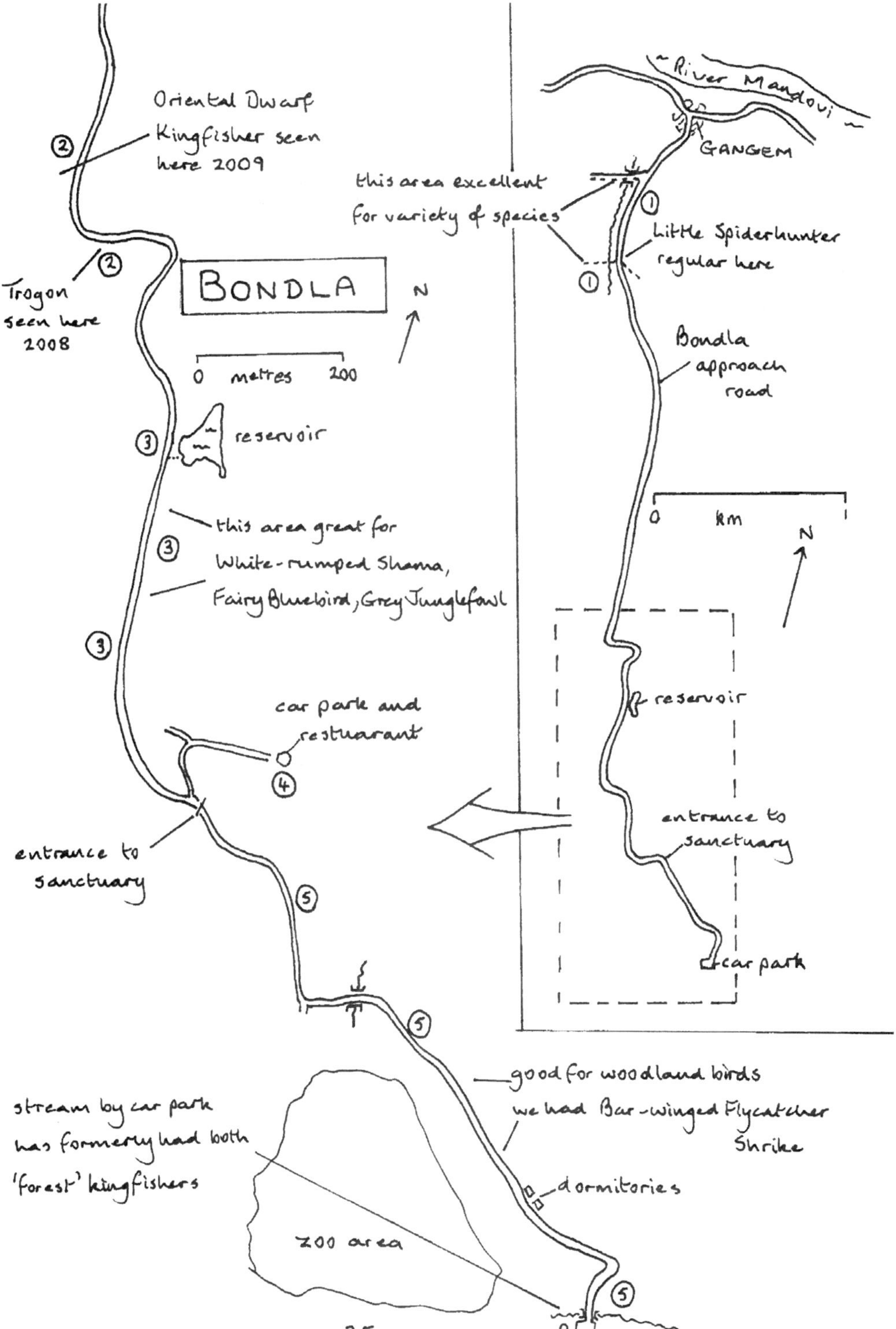
BONDLA
N
0 metres 200
Oriental Dwarf Kingfisher seen here 2009
2
Trogon seen here 2008
3
reservoir
this area great for White-rumped Shama, Fairy Bluebird, Grey Junglefowl
car park and restuarant
4
entrance to sanctuary
5
good for woodland birds
we had Bar-winged Flycatcher Shrike
stream by car park has formerly had both 'forest' kingfishers
dormitories
zoo area
P
River Mandovi
GANGEM
this area excellent for variety of species
1
Little Spiderhunter regular here
Bondla approach road
0 km
reservoir
entrance to sanctuary
car park

there have included Forest Wagtail, Indian Pitta (near the dormitories) and both Oriental Dwarf Kingfisher and Blue-eared Kingfisher (on the stream by the car park).

Other species reported at Bondla have included Indian Scimitar Babbler, Black Eagle, Blue-bearded Bee-eater, Emerald Dove, Blue-faced Malkoha, Banded Bay Cuckoo, Sri Lankan Frogmouth, Large-billed Leaf Warbler and Speckled Piculet.